THE HISTORY

HENRYS RECORDS

Southampton's finest record store

1956-1988

By

John Clare

Additional material by David St John

Front cover: Henry at 116 St Marys Street Southampton

©JohnClare/David St John 2021

COPYRIGHT

All rights reserved. No part of this publication may be reproduced, stored in a retrieval system, or transmitted in any form or by any means, electronic, electrostatic, recording, magnetic tape, mechanical, photocopying or otherwise, without prior permission in writing from the publishers. The publishers make no representation, express or implied, with regard to the accuracy of the information contained within this publication and cannot accept any responsibility in law for any errors or omissions.

The publishers have made every reasonable effort to trace the copyright owners of any image contained in this book. In the event of any omission, the publishers will be pleased to hear from anyone who has not been appropriately acknowledged, and to make a correction in any further reprints and publications. The images throughout this book are from the author's personal photographs collection but credits can be given upon receiving validated sources. Many of the photos are reproduced in original colour when downloading the digital e-book version of this same publication.

Published by DSJP (David St John Publishing) 2021

www.davidstjohn.co.uk

www.davidstjohn.co.uk/henrys.html

The right of John Clare to be identified as author of this Work has been asserted by him in accordance with sections 77 and 78 of the Copyright, Designs and Patent Act 1988.

DEDICATION

I dedicate this book to Linda, my wife of 35 years. You will read how and where we met in this book when our paths crossed for the first time. If my life had been different, then we would have not had our precious children nor moved to the glorious state of Western Australia!

This recent photo at our daughter's beach front house overlooking the Indian Ocean – a real taste of Paradise.

In addition, I dedicate it to the memory of a very special person, whose own story began over one hundred years ago in South Wales. Like me, he followed his own dream of running a music store - the dream came true when the family decided to move to Southampton, leading to the 1956 opening of a record shop that soon became established as one of the finest in the South. My own dream came true in 1969, landing a job as a young assistant alongside this great character. Henry's Records is still fondly remembered, the shop having closed its shutters in 1988 but takes its place as a landmark in the city as part of its modern history and heritage. Little did I know where it would end up within a few years. I hope you will enjoy reading my story as much as I have in writing it all.

Henry Sansom 1917-1993

CONTENTS   Page

FOREWORD. David St John

CHAPTER 1.   The Early Years - South Wales……………………..1

CHAPTER 2-   Dunn's Music Stores Cardiff………………….…….3

CHAPTER 3.   Henry's Records opens in Southampton…………..13

CHAPTER 4.   Henry's Records new premises…………………....29

CHAPTER 5.   The John Clare Years 1969 onwards………..….…41

CHAPTER 6.   The Jocks- some of the many popular DJs………..51

CHAPTER 7.   The Seventies – changes…………………………..62

CHAPTER 8.   21st Anniversary…………………………………....77

CHAPTER 9.   The Eighties – Vinyl takes a dip…………………..91

CHAPTER 10. The end of an era………………………………….106

CHAPTER 11. A life-changing decision………………………….113

CHAPTER 12. Acknowledgements………………………..……...117

CHAPTER 13. What happened next………………………………124

CHAPTER 14. A big turnaround…………………………………..129

CHAPTER 15. The next phase……………………………….…,.133

CHAPTER 16. Thanks for the memories…………………………136

APPENDIX.   Miscellaneous……………………………………...139

FOREWORD - DAVID ST JOHN

Most of us had dreams from an early age, generally throughout our school years as we learnt more about the world, and all that it offers. We also enjoyed our young hobbies and pastimes, some of which we grew out of in our teenage period. Stamp collecting, pen-friends, train-spotting, comics and the like were popular in the Fifties, until a new wave of music made a major impact on our lives if growing up in that decade. We never knew what lay ahead in our formative years, but some of us were very lucky to pursue a career that was created out of a passion. Many people end up in dead-end jobs, often following in their parents' footsteps or for a variety of other reasons. They may well spend the rest of their working years in well-paid employment with a comfortable life, albeit with a degree of boredom and regrets.

This wonderful story starts over a hundred years ago in 1917, with the birth of Henry Sansom into a Welsh family. He was blessed with a musical ear that would later see him play piano and church organ in his home city of Cardiff, as well as instilling a passion for record shops. By the age of eleven, he was helping out in a local music store which gave him the idea of one day running his own shop. This dream eventually came true a few years later, as the family made the big decision to better themselves by moving to the South Coast of England, offering the chance of decent employment during the austere post-war years.

As a young lad growing up in Southampton around the same time, I was well into pop music from an early age, spending many hours in local record shops. Everybody knew that the best record store was located in St Mary Street, not far from the city centre just across the road from the busy open-air Kingsland Market. The late Sixties saw me working for Reg Bicknell at Revis Automatics, an amusement machine company which sold and serviced fruit machines, pintables and jukeboxes. Like many businesses, Revis had an account with Henry's Records, regularly replenishing the records as they went in and out of the charts. The shop atmosphere was a treat for us music fans, carrying a wide range of music to suit all tastes, thanks to the knowledgeable staff. Then, in the summer of '69 (cue for a song) a new member joined the team – a self-confessed 'vinyl junkie' by the name of fifteen year old John Clare, whose amazing passion for music and knowledge would soon elevate Henry's Records into the top range of record stores in the South. Its reputation is still remembered to this day – better still we now have the opportunity to read all about the glory days.

John was an intelligent grammar schoolboy who decided to drop out of the system, much to the consternation of his parents and teachers who naturally hoped to see him carry on with further education. He spent most of his pocket money on records during the early Sixties, as the charts were full of the most diverse music imaginable. Many 'baby boomers' can remember poring over the boxes and shelves of 45s and L.P.s in their local record stores. Then asking the staff to place their selection on the turntables, feeding the sounds into the nearby listening booths. This only applied to singles of course, most of which lasted about two to three minutes, but it was good to 'try before you buy'. Albums offered much more, as we bought our LPs, often lured by the cover artwork and photographs of our favourite artistes of the day. The next stage was to take them home, read the notes on the back with the play-list, followed by the magic moment we took the record out of the sleeve, smell it, before gently placing it down on our own record players, lowering the stylus onto the plastic.

Many of us owned the basic Dansette for playing the singles or albums one at a time, unless we had the better 'auto-change' model with a spindle, allowing us to load a few more discs. Then, as each record played out, the arm would lift and return to the side as the next disc dropped down to start the next playback. What a moment when that needle dropped down on side one of an album, leading us into the first track of new unheard songs – nothing to beat it! No wonder that sales of 'retro' vinyl records have exploded in recent years, including re-releases of classic albums that are now played on expensive state of the art turntables through top quality hi-fi equipment. Current 'streaming' music and downloads pale into insignificance when looking back at the experiences enjoyed by early record buyers with their 'hands on' recollections.

As you read John's own memoirs, you will soon realise that he was following in similar footsteps of Henry himself, later becoming more of close family than mere staff. Within a very short time, John Clare's name was well known as he knew the music business inside out, with a canny knowledge and foresight when it came to knowing what the public wanted. Any obscure request would see him get to work on finding any record, label or artiste, without the use of the internet that we all take for granted nowadays. I often called by to have a look through the racks, plus a little chat with him, in between his non-stop serving at the counter. It was busy all through the day with customers, local musicians plus the popular disc jockeys who just enjoyed 'talking shop'. I left Southampton in 1972 but have kept in touch with my pals ever since, many of them being featured on my website across several pages featuring the groups from the late Fifties on. My first webpage told of my own days as lead singer with local bands, followed by several more dedicated pages thanks to people getting in touch to share their own memories in words and rare photos.

Around the early Eighties, I was well aware of the existence of a massive collection of information on Hampshire groups, contained in a large ring-binder full of hand-written A4 sheets. 'Southern Roots' was the brainchild of John Clare, assisted by his pal Terry Hounsome, taking over two years of research and writing – a real 'labour of love' to coin the cliché. They had gone to live shows all over the area to meet and talk with the musicians, as well as phoning around in order to gain as much information that was catalogued in this mini-encyclopaedia. I had been sent a small typed condensed version of SR, thanks to my former band-mate Beau, having played together in our first group back in 1964. He had kindly sent me a rare photo of our later 1965 band, being the very first image that kick-started the rest of my many 60s music web-pages. I had always kept in touch with John, who enjoyed my new sharing outlet on the Southampton scene, followed by his grand gesture of sending me the heavy SR files, at great expense back over from Australia to the UK for safe keeping. It gave me the opportunity to use the in-depth descriptions of several well-known groups as well as including many rare photos. These pages have grown over the years, with thousands of 'hits' and much more input.

The 'Southern Roots' files have played a pivotal part in helping me to write successive web-pages named 'Call Up the Groups' as a little nod to the Barron Knights who released great mickey-takes of the early 60s pop groups. The background information and fascinating photos have enhanced it all, as well as leading to my setting up that very first 'Back to the Sixties' show at the Concorde Club back in 2008. I had several 'vintage' musicians who were still performing in various local groups so it clicked in to set the wheels in motion for the annual reunion shows – reports can be seen on my relevant web-pages. Several suggestions came my way as regards transposing much of the content into book form as a more permanent way to publish it away from the internet. I have been working on a draft copy for some while, following on from my other books in the last couple of years, whilst recently publishing two books that link in to the whole story.

'Southern Roots : Part 1 – A Rock'n'Roll Story 1958-1972' is an autobiographical account of my own early years on the stage, later to be followed by a second book that carries on with my solo comedy career and much more. Before that, I will be publishing 'Southern Root - Part 2' which offers more in-depth information on many of the featured names spread across my website, along with many unseen old photos of the leading groups, singers, DJs, venues and all that went with the main Sixties era. Another book has been published, having been sent copies of three magazines that were produced by Avenue Artistes back in 1963/64 as an in-house publicity drive. I have reproduced every page of the three issues, containing reports of the local acts and dance halls that they appeared in. A nostalgic look at what it was all about at that exciting time as Beatlemania was taking over the pop music scene. 'The Southern Entertainer' can be found on my Amazon author page, also linked to Henry's Records. The musicians would buy the latest chart hits, then dash home to learn the chords and lyrics in readiness for their live gigs. The DJs spending a lot more to add to their ever growing collection to keep their own audiences dancing the night away, often appearing alongside the groups to make for a terrific night out.

John had written down a basic draft of 'The History of Henry's Records' many years ago – just for the fun of it with no major intentions of publishing it anywhere. I therefore recently suggested that he send me a copy along with any of his personal photos as it would make for an interesting book. It has been a wonderful experience to read and edit slight parts of the whole story, ready to be enjoyed by a wider audience. You will read about the highs and lows of his working and personal life, which took many turns, but working out so well in the end. His time at Henry's Records gave him a grounding in the business world, from a small shop leading to his later years, as his experience led to positions within a multi-million dollar corporate outlet in the beautiful city of Perth Australia. It nearly all went drastically wrong for him and his family on a few occasions, but Lady Luck intervened as you will learn. Southampton has a rich history with several landmarks all over the city, including the Royal Pier, Civic Centre buildings, Docks and many more. The mid Fifties saw another added to the list, with the advent of this wonderful record shop that holds many memories for staff, customers and all that knew the St Marys area back in its heyday. Naturally, some old photos have suffered from the lack of quality when reproduced but they do highlight much of the relevant content.

I am sure you will enjoy this book as much as I have, thanks to another fellow Sotonian, with whom I share 'southern roots'.

David St John April 2021

CHAPTER ONE: THE EARLY YEARS
SOUTH WALES

JOHN CLARE WRITES:

Henry John Sansom was born in South Wales on 28th August 1917 at 119 Cyfartha Street in Cardiff to Albert, a Welsh miner and Rose nee Lynham, originally from Bridgewater Somerset. She had been working in the Collar Factory, living in a little flat above a shop with her two elder sisters, Mabe and Em. They had met while Albert had been on a visit to Bridgewater, with Rose soon moving to Cardiff, where they got married in 1915. There was little work in Bridgewater, so she was more than happy to move to the big city, where she first went into service before working on the trams. Albert served in the Great War 1914-1918.

Albert and Rose Sansom

Baby Henry

Henry was a small, very delicate boy, often falling ill as much as once a fortnight, gazing out of his bedroom window, with people saying that he looked like a ghost! He even had his tonsils out at home, being too frail to have the operation undertaken in hospital as doctors feared that it would kill him. The Sansoms were quite poor, leading Albert to resort to all sorts of entrepreneurial ideas, in order to get money to feed the family. He would hire out bikes, make homemade scooters and 'Felix the Cat' push-along toys. Many of these being sold on Cardiff station before catching the local train to the coal pit. Rose made other ends meet by making sweets, as well as dress making for the neighbours. Their only form of entertainment in the evenings was playing cards, or having a sing-a-long, but as soon as they had some spare money, they bought an old wind-up gramophone. This is when Henry's obsession with music began, fascinated by the sounds of the records emanating from the large horn, a sign of things to come.

CHAPTER TWO: DUNN'S MUSIC STORES CARDIFF

In 1921, a young man by the name of John Dunn, working for Waddington's pianos was transferred to the Cardiff branch of that store. Also working at the Cardiff shop was a young French polisher named Harry Lambert, who was married to Henry's Auntie Em. Harry had met Dunn before while serving in the army in WW1, and it was not long before he became a friend of the whole Sansom/Lynham family. In 1924, having worked with pianos and being fairly musical, he decided to open a music store. It was to be the first of a small chain called Dunn's Music Stores. The first one was at 53 Clifton Street, Cardiff. Henry's mother and father were asked if they'd like to run it for him. Thus, the Sansoms moved when Henry was seven years old to live above the shop where his legacy of involvement in record shops began. The shop had no back entrance and no bathroom but did have a tiny back garden.

Dunn's Music Store Barry Cardiff

Em and Harry Lambert

Henry was then attending St Anne's school in Croft Street, a quaint little old fashioned Victorian school with a small church alongside - still there today in much of its original form. One of Henry's favourite pastimes at this time was to visit Jones's sweetshop on the corner of Croft St to spend a ha'penny on some sweets. He would often look through all the sweets that Mr Jones had on offer and then leave without buying anything, crossing the street to go into Patton's and do the same thing! His shrewdness with money would become a lifetime practice! The record business in those days was quite interesting. One of the biggest Music Hall acts of the 1920s being the Two Gilberts who had several hits. including 'Ukulele Lady' and 'Yes, We Have No Bananas'. This rare image shows that Tom Gilbert released his own solo version in amongst their own recordings.

'Ukulele Lady' by Tom Gilbert (baritone) on 78 rpm

   Mr. Dunn used to purchase his records from Tilley's warehouse in Wood St. They stocked all record labels except Decca, but mainly Columbia, Parlophone, HMV and Regal Zonophone. Decca's warehouse was in Charles St. Henry's father built a type of billy-cart truck in which he would load all of the 78s and push them back to Clifton St. In 1927, business in Clifton St had been going so well that Dunn decided to open another shop in Barry Island at 21 Holton Road which he purchased from a piano teacher called Nellie Williams, who was later to teach young Henry to play. The Sansom family then moved up from Cardiff to run it, being replaced at Clifton St by Henry's Uncle Harry Lambert & Auntie Em, his mother's eldest sister.

Nellie Williams – piano teacher

John Dunn with a beloved pet

21 Holton Road Barry- formerly Dunn's Music Shop

Business boomed in Barry Island - a town that was wide open for opportunity, and the only competitor selling records was a little greengrocer shop in Lower Pike St which sold the strange combination of ice cream, fruit and vegetables and gramophone records! However, they didn't last long once the Dunn organization had set up. Then Dunn did a very odd thing, opening a second shop in Barry Island in the same thoroughfare at no. 29 Holton Road, just to be in the middle of the street! Henry's youngest Aunt, Gladys was put in to run this one. The upstairs was rented out to a fortune teller and Gladys would often see women departing in floods of tears after being told some prophecy of the future that they would rather have not heard! One of Gladys's most famous customers was the then current heavyweight boxing champion of Great Britain, Jack Peterson. He used to ask Gladys out to stroll through the local Porth Kerry Park, where he used to train for upcoming fights, by running up and down the lengthy wooden staircase that led up through the woods to the cliff top.

   The 11-year-old Henry (above) had started to let music become the dominant force in his life. Taking piano lessons from Miss Nellie Williams upstairs helped him to eventually play the organ at Methyr Dyfan church, where he sang in the choir in between ringing the bells. He helped his parents out by working in Dunn's music store on Saturdays. Henry was attending Gladstone Rd Secondary School during this time, where a teacher with a notorious reputation for his severe discipline called 'Scratchy' Harris became his favourite teacher.

Recognizing Henry's interest in music, he would invite him to his house to listen to his extensive classical 78 collection. Around this time, Henry met two of his greatest friends in life, Cyril Blake and Howard Hook. The three friends would spend many hours upstairs at the Barry Island shop listening to music and in particular, several versions of the same aria sung by various different tenors to compare and discuss the merits of the different interpretations by each of them.

Henry was now playing an active part as sales assistant in his parent's shop. One of his more strenuous duties was as a delivery boy. He would have to go from Barry to Cardiff, sometimes by bus, sometimes by train and then to Tilley's and Charles St to collect stock, then cart them all the way back, which considering the weight of 78s was no joke but had to be done, if a living was to be made. The bus from Cardiff to Barry in those days travelled along a tiny narrow road on a cliff top with a sheer drop on one side, having no streetlights whatsoever. It is now a large dual carriageway and extremely well lit. The one advantage of collecting the stock by bus was that the bus used to stop right outside the shop. If he went by train, it meant carrying the 78s home from Barry station. Gladys was long suffering from delivering records to her shop. She would somehow bring four boxes of fragile discs from the warehouse, balanced on the handlebars of her bicycle whilst cycling with one hand on the handlebars and one hand on top of the records. It was extremely heavy going when cycling uphill - I don't think that modern Health and Safety regulations would quite allow it now!

Naturally, if they fell and smashed, it was a lot of money lost. Once the records had been delivered, it was nowhere near as easy to sell them as it became in the boom 60s and 70s years. For a start, there were no paper bags for customers to take them home in, as they were too expensive, although most record shops of the day, including Dunn's had their own cardboard sleeves to insert the 78s, with the name of the shop advertised on the front. For a customer to take the record home, it would not only have to be put into the cardboard sleeve, but then wrapped in brown paper with cardboard stuffing, ending up with string tied around it. You can imagine that it took a long time to sell one record and invariably, the customer would bring it back and complain that it was broken. The usual logical cause of this was because the customer had tried to pull the string off instead of cutting it, although they would never admit it, so long arguments would develop. Customers used to listen to records in the shop, being the cause for a lot more bother than it is in recent times when you just put a CD in and press a button, or simply listen on a mobile phone. For every new record played, the gramophone had to be wound up and the needle changed. Dunn's Barry Island music store had four wind-up gramophones for customers to listen to records on, one in the front of the shop, one in the middle, one in the back room and incredibly, one in the kitchen! Customers actually used to sit in the kitchen with a cup of tea and listen to records!

John Dunn opened his fourth shop in 1935 at 229 – 231 Cowbridge Rd in Cardiff. Harry and Em were then relocated from Clifton St to run it, with Dunn overseeing Clifton St. Before that, Dunn had been mainly involved in the repair side of the business, repairing windup gramophones. He was a very heavy drinker, knocking back half a bottle of whisky a day, having the temper of a wild bull. If he had trouble getting a new spring into a gramophone, he would just explode and throw the whole thing up the garden, usually doing damage to the customer's property and having to replace it! If no damage had been done, Gladys usually took over to finish the job with no fuss at all. However, the booming business wouldn't last. As the Second World War approached and rationing started, limiting people's spending power, the business started going downhill fast and the accounts side of things was getting on top of Dunn, never being very good at figures. He hired an accountant from Stroud, a Mr. Burr to sort out the financial mess. Before Dunn knew where he was, Burr said to close the two shops in Cardiff and sack all the staff. Rose, Albert and Gladys were begrudgingly kicked out of the two Barry shops and Dunn ran one and Burr the other, eventually closing 21 Holton Road as well. Then Burr cleverly engineered a takeover, completely gazumping Dunn. With the depression that followed, no money to take Burr to court, Dunn had a stroke at sixty years of age. He got over the stroke, but never really got over losing his business. He lived to be eighty but died penniless, with no family of his own in Godalming Surrey. By this time, the seeds of passion for music had been sown in young Henry. He went off to The Royal Academy of Music where he soon gained his licentiate, but mainly dreamed of running his own record shop one day.

Graduation Day

CHAPTER THREE: HENRYS RECORDS OPENS IN SOUTHAMPTON

By 1939, the Second World War had broken out, seeing Henry called up to serve for his country, like most young men. Luckily, he never saw any dangerous action, spending most of his time operating searchlights on the Kentish coast. Post-war times were tough, the record shops having mostly disappeared, leaving a bleak outlook for the Sansom family finances. The work prospects were fairly slim in South Wales, as well as Albert not wishing to return to the mines at his age, so they all decided to make a fresh start elsewhere. The family relocated to Eastleigh, near Southampton as the job market was more forthcoming, especially with the railway works there and opportunities in the automobile industry. The better weather was another bonus, as well as being near the Solent and the New Forests

Rose's extended family followed as well, except for the youngest son Fred and wife Phyllis, who stayed back in Cardiff. Henry's first job at Waller's grocery shop, was soon followed by landing a plum vacancy at the nearby Bennett's Music store, part of a large chain of shops that sold musical instruments, particularly specializing in pianos. Mainly Portsmouth-based, in addition to selling records, sheet music and musical equipment. It was here that he got to know some of the record company travelling salesmen extremely well, leading to the start of the idea of opening his very own music store. Henry was taking it all in, picking brains as he gradually learned as much as he could about the business structure. Evenings saw him playing piano in local pubs, enabling him to save enough money to see his dreams turn into reality.

The next photos show the male and female family groups – a mix of uncles and cousins in Eastleigh (except Fred) with Henry's father Albert on the back row (4th left). John Dunn on front row (1st left). Young lads at the front being Jackie and Norman.

Then with the ladies showing Henry's mother front centre (with Nanny Gould's arm around her right shoulder). The little girl in front of her is her daughter Jeannette, Henry's sister and Linda's Mum. She was much younger than Henry because she wasn't planned!

Waller & Co Fruit and Veg Shop

As mentioned, the above photo shows Henry and pal – or maybe a fellow shop-worker in front of the old Waller store. This first employment gave him another chance to learn about retail although his heart naturally needed to get back into a music outlet.

Another rare image shows Henry beaming away as part of the Bennett staff photo, with fond memories of his time with the company.

Bennetts' staff

Finally, after a great deal of encouragement from the then EMI Regional Manager, and good friend Dennis Tungate, Henry found premises at 136 St Mary Street in Southampton, on the corner with James Street. The rent was £250 a year (around £4,500 in today's money) plus rates, with the first 'HENRY'S RECORDS' seeing the light of day on Saturday November 23rd, 1956 with a capital outlay of £500. The opening stock consisted of a £150 opening order from Thompson, Diamond and Butcher, one of the major record distributors of the day who gave him credit facilities on a month-to-month basis. In addition, Dennis Tungate had helped Henry to negotiate a smaller than normal opening order of £150 with the lucrative HMV agency, which was hard to obtain in those days, especially for a small new outlet.

136 St Marys Street 1956

The first day's record stock comprised of seventy five LPs, fifty E.P.s and three hundred 78s, the latter gradually replaced by the new hard-wearing vinyl discs that were taking off in the middle of the decade. The other stock included a £16 record player purchased from J.J. Storie, £8 worth of toys from Rood Brothers, £30 worth of musical goods from Rosetti & Co. plus £4 worth of sheet music from Francis, Day and Hunter. Henry had no staff, just himself, putting his own personal radiogram in the shop for customers to listen to records on. He did have some occasional help from his mother, Rose, Aunty Gladys and her husband Bill Lewis, along with Uncle Harry Lambert, especially around that first Christmas. Harry built a lot of the store's fixtures and fittings, thus saving more money in these tight times which helped immensely.

136 interior

On that first Saturday, Henry took £25.8s 6d and for the first full week, he took £178.5s.9d. The prices of records were 5s.6d for a 78, 9s.6d for an EP, £1.12s.6d for an LP and £1.18s for a classical LP. Thankfully, a young American by the name of Elvis Presley had broken big, earlier that year in May with his first 78 release of 'Heartbreak Hotel', spearheading the rock and roll boom, so the timing for opening a record shop was perfect! This amazing record still sounds good to this day, as well as inspiring a new wave of young pop singers and musicians during the late Fifties.

'Heartbreak Hotel'

St Marys Street 1950s

Record stocks could only be ordered from the retail outlets by post at that time. There were no phone orders, let alone the luxury of our modern internet facilities. The orders were then delivered by Royal Mail by train or Post Office vans (no couriers in the Fifties). Therefore, several trips had to be made by Henry himself to the main Southampton railway station parcel pick up office to collect large quantities of records. These were then brought back to the shop to keep the stock levels up. Henry's mother and Auntie Gladys would again be minding the family shop while Henry was at the station.

Two weeks after opening, Henry was introduced to someone who was to be a great help in promoting his shop over the next couple of years. There was a tailors' store up the road in St Mary's Street called Sydney's Men's Outfitters, owned by one Sydney Shock, who just happened to be the brother-in-law of singer Frankie Vaughan, currently riding high in the chart with his cover version of the American hit song by Jim Lowe - 'Green Door'. Sydney had got to know Henry pretty well during the first couple of weeks that he'd been open and Frankie was due in town for a concert. Frankie obviously dropped in to say hello to his brother-in-law, Sydney taking the opportunity to take Frankie down the road and introduce him to the new record shop owner. This caught Henry quite by surprise, but Frankie was not amused to see the original Jim Lowe version of his current hit, being prominently promoted in Henry's front window! However, a friendship developed, leading to Frankie making two or three officially promoted personal appearances at the shop over the next couple of years. This caused gridlocks all over St Mary Street whenever this major star rolled up, as he was topping the bill at the Gaumont Theatre.

1957 Frankie Vaughan fans block the road

The first outing was in September 1957 to promote his new single 'Wanderin' Eyes'– the follow up to his No. 1 hit earlier that year- 'The Garden Of Eden' 'Wanderin' Eyes' eventually peaked at no 6 in the chart, but on this very day in September, it had just been released, so fans could not only buy it for the first time but then actually meet the man that sang it and get him to autograph their precious copy. Henry had ordered in one hundred and fifty various Frankie Vaughan 78s, selling them all on the day, in the noisy packed shop. Overwhelmed by the numbers, they had to introduce a one-way system as the eager customers had to use the back door, allowing in a few at a time. They were then ushered out of the main front door, clutching their precious purchases. Who knows how many of these discs still exist?

More fans outside the besieged shop

Frankie Vaughan and Henry

Other popular big name artists of the day who combined their local show appearances with promotional visits included the likes of Ronnie Hilton, Gerry Brereton, Max Bygraves, Fred Emney, Russ Conway, and a few by local star, a former milkman from the local Isle of Wight - Craig Douglas.

Craig Douglas

Craig Douglas

Business was beginning to pick up significantly, so much so, that Henry could no longer run the shop on his own with occasional help from the relatives, thus needing an assistant. The first was a girl whose name is sadly lost in time, being followed by a young man called Ken Court who was to stay for the next two years. Things were building rapidly, encouraging Henry to expand his customer base even more by advertising regularly in the Southampton 'What's On' Guide.

First assistant – now in her Eighties?

Ken Court

Finally, business had improved beyond all expectations, leading to a short move to bigger premises just ten doors up the road to 116 St Mary Street on the 18th May 1958. Henry's Records remained at the same location for the next thirty years, establishing itself as the best record shop in the South. The old corner premises at no. 136 were taken over by local impresario Reg Calvert, who had moved down from Yorkshire just a few years before. Apart from working as a hairdresser by day, Reg was an accomplished piano player/compere by night, appearing in local pubs and clubs. He was one of the earliest disc jockeys, filling in between the dance band's sessions by playing the new rock'n'roll records, naturally purchased from Henry's shop. Reg booked and managed several groups and singers, including his own stable of 'tribute' artistes such as Elvis, Cliff, Buddy and others who looked and sounded like the real thing. This was way before the same genre kicked off in the Eighties, being very innovative as a pioneer in this field. One of his early managed acts was singer/musician Rory Blackwell who gained a Guinness World Record for an eighty four hour drumming marathon attempt at the newly-named Bandbox in 1960. The building was previously known as the jazz-based Ace of Clubs before the latest pop music era swept in at that exciting time.

This photo shows the Calvert-inspired publicity stunt in full flow, attracting local and national press.

Rory Blackwell drumming marathon with adoring fans

The Bandbox

Calvert later moved to Rugby, setting up home at Clifton Hall where he launched 'The School of Rock'n'Roll', as a training ground for the new bands to improve their skills, backed by Reg's great flair for publicity. He later moved into pirate radio by launching Radio Sutch (as in Screaming Lord) but met a tragic end in 1966 when being shot by a former business colleague.

The Relocation Sale

CHAPTER FOUR: HENRY'S RECORDS NEW PREMISES

116 St Marys Street

After the success of the first shop, no expense was spared on fitting out 116, partly because Henry had bought the leasehold, therefore owning the property outright. All new fittings and fixtures were ordered, partly sponsored by EMI and Decca. The shop was three times the size of 136, enabling Henry to not only quadruple his range of records but managing to add a significant range of record carrying cases, record cleaning accessories, styli, musical instruments, sheet music, radiograms and small electrical goods like transistor radios, kettles and toasters. Along with the new look shop and more professional fittings, Henry decided it was time to have his own bag for customers and although a very economical brown paper variety, it was the first of many more creative designs to follow in later years

The new premises

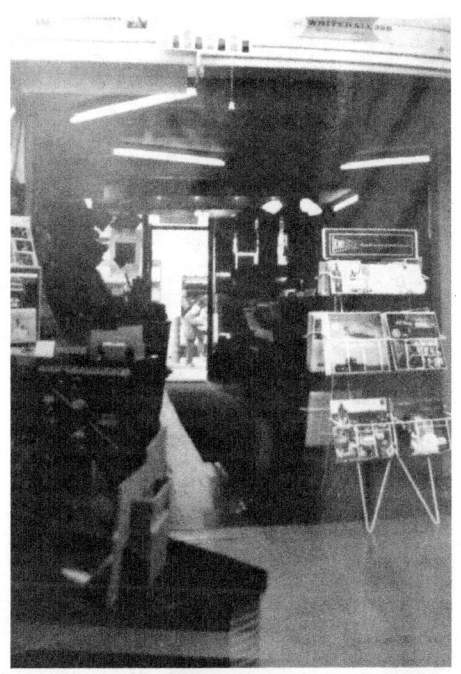

116 interior

In 1960, another significant development happened in the record business. Up to that point, none of the big American labels had their own independent distribution in England, being licensed to the big three UK companies, EMI, Decca and Philips. Elvis Presley's RCA recordings and all other same label recording artists were released on

EMI's turquoise blue HMV label. Other American labels such as Monument, Atlantic, Dot, Specialty, Laurie and United Artists were released on Decca's London American label, with the American Columbia label (which had to call itself C.B.S. in England because EMI already had a label called Columbia and owned the copyright) was released on Philips. But in 1958, Warner Brothers, the big movie studio decided to launch its own record label, thus becoming the first U.S. company to organize its own independent distribution via a wholesaler called Selecta. It wasn't long before other U.S. giants followed suit with RCA setting up a distribution deal with Decca and Mercury with Philips. Warner featured such top name artists as the Everly Brothers, Bing Crosby, Tab Hunter etc. The Everlys' 'Cathy's Clown' was the first release with the ground-breaking number of WB 45 -1.

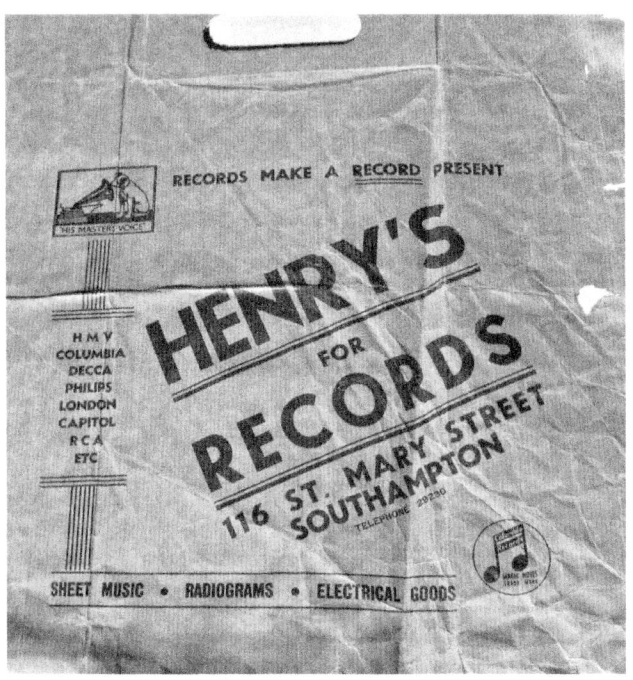

Ken Court departed in 1960, replaced by a new assistant, Reginald Mann, who concentrated on the electrical side of the business, being his field of expertise. The store was then able to offer a lucrative repair business. Reginald was to stay with Henry for the next six years until 1966 when the staff expanded to three with the addition of Mr Mann's daughter, Jenny.

Reg Mann

Listening Booths

The personal appearances by popular recording artists of the day continued and in March 1964, Henry pulled off a massive coup. There was quite a bit of interest in a new form of music coming out of Jamaica called bluebeat or ska, predominantly being brought into the country and distributed by white Jamaican, Chris Blackwell, who was later to form his own record label. Island Records. At that time, he had negotiated a distribution deal through Fontana records, a subsidiary of Philips. Blackwell had already had some mild success with the likes of Duke Reid, Lesley Kong, Sir Coxsone Dodd and other artistes, who were creating massive interest within the new 'Mod' culture, whose spending power on clothes, scooters and especially records helped Henry's balance sheets. Southampton had a strong Caribbean community by this time, helping to boost sales of the music as most record shops did not stock these rare discs.

Early in 1964, Blackwell hit the jackpot with a fifteen year old Jamaican singer Millie (Small) whose release 'My Boy Lollipop' was racing up the charts. Philips offered Henry a personal appearance at his shop, taking place on the very same week that the record hit the No. 2 spot in the national Top 40. The result of this being huge crowds gathering on the day for a 'Meet and Greet' session with Millie, who signed copies of the disc for several hours. This resulted in the police having to seal off both ends of the street, as no traffic could get through the crowds of fans all over the road and pavements.

I wonder if any readers can identify themselves or their relatives who in these photographs? A great day that was talked about for a long time after, although Millie was never able to follow up the success of this brilliant hit that still resonates at parties and disco nights to this day. Even the youngsters sing along to this infectious sound that was enjoyed by their grandparents in the day!

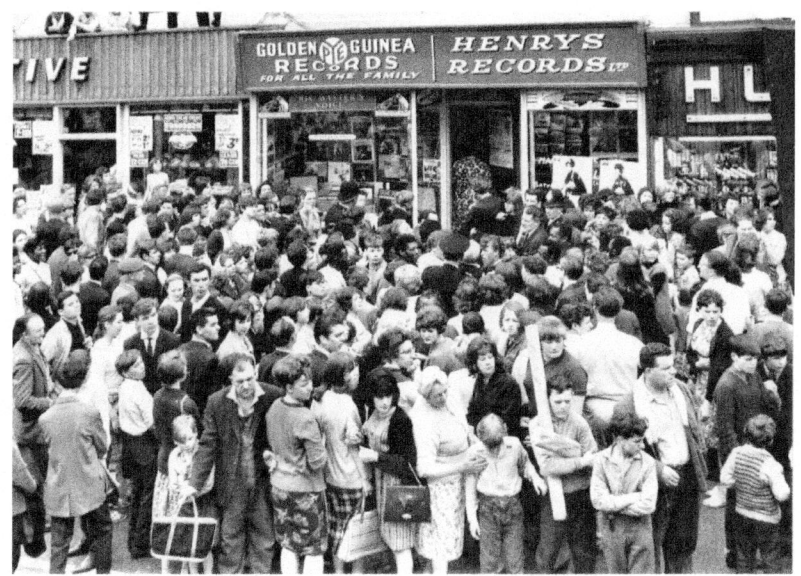
Millie Mania!

1967 heralded in the 'Summer of Love' as a huge music revolution was taking place, spearheaded by The Beatles' 'Sgt Pepper' album. Newer weird and wonderful sounds came out of Los Angeles and San Francisco as the new 'hippy' movement influenced the groups on this side of the Atlantic, mirrored in their own song-writing and recordings. Reggae/Bluebeat/Ska was still selling well, along with the new exciting Atlantic/Stax/Tamla Motown sounds. Bob Dylan had influenced many up-and-coming artistes, whose cover versions featured heavily in the charts. Record sales were now phenomenal, and it took a lot to keep in touch with the new sounds that were now in demand from Britain's youth. Reg Mann, realizing that keeping up with the new chart trends was out of his depth, decided to bow out to be replaced by Peter Batt whose own electrical knowledge kept the busy repair side in good stead. Henry knew that he needed a younger element to help out with choosing the right kind of music, leading to a succession of teenagers added to the staff - one of the better ones being his own niece Linda who, unbeknown to me, would later become a very important part of my personal life journey.

Millie welcomed by Linda (the future Mrs Clare)

By 1968, Henry was ordering new albums by top artists such as the Beatles and Rolling Stones in quantities of 500 and selling out in a week! The Beatles white double album caused a particularly annoying workload, caused by the four colour photos of each member of the group, with accompanying giant poster all coming separately. This then resulted in some 'lucky' staff member having to undertake the boring job of inserting them all into the five hundred LP covers! During this time, Henry started another vigorous advertising campaign, utilising the Southern Evening Echo to fend off fierce competition from the rival record shops in town, including Francis Records in Pound Tree Rd, Spikins of Woolston, Suttons in Shirley High St and Southern Radio in Portswood Junction plus the new emerging threat from newsagent/bookseller, W.H. Smith and Boots the Chemist. In one advert that appeared in the Echo in December 1968, Henry decided to plug the new single by one 'Eddie Swann'. Who was Eddie Swann? None other than Sydney of Sydney's Men's Outfitters who had decided that if his brother-in-law, Frankie Vaughan could be a star then so could he, landing himself a recording contract with the small independent Morgan label. Sadly, a star he was not destined to be, so back to tailoring!

The personal in-store appearances continued throughout the mid-Sixties, including visits by Cat Stevens, promoting his first single of 'I Love My Dog', Solomon King with 'She Wears My Ring' and the Love Affair who were No.1 at the time with 'Rainbow Valley', the follow-up to their previous No.1 'Everlasting Love'. Their ecstatic, young female fans nearly wrecked the shop in an effort get close to their latest idols.

Love Affair promotion

CHAPTER FIVE: THE JOHN CLARE YEARS 1969 ONWARDS

June 1969 is the part of the story where I come in, as a fifteen-year-old music fanatic, whose pocket money savings from a newspaper round from the age of twelve allowed me to spend much of it on buying all five of the main music papers of the time. Still at school, I jumped on my bike to cover the early morning, evening and weekend rounds in order to feed my 'addiction'. The Melody Maker, New Musical Express, Record Mirror, Sounds and Disc/Music Echo were all read and studied cover to cover. This gave me an extensive knowledge of the record industry as well as learning about the more specialised fields of music such as jazz, folk, blues, soul, reggae, C&W and much more outside the main pop music side. Any spare money left over from buying the papers was spent on records, usually second-hand, as I couldn't afford new. My dream had always been to work in the music industry, planning to go to university, get a B.A. degree, then become a journalist in the field.

I envisaged myself writing for one of those five main papers that I avidly read cover to cover, where I could interview all of my heroes. There was just one snag……. I hated school, and after failing my maths 'O' level and not being able to progress to 'A's until I did it again, I was looking for a way out – and then I found it by chance. I just noticed a small advert in the Echo, inserted by Henry's Record Shop, looking for a sales assistant! I was already familiar with the shop as my best mate at school, Ian Derham, lived just off of St Mary's Rd and we had often nipped into Henry's on the way home to his place after school at Taunton's Grammar school.

It was, even then, easily the most fantastic record shop that I had ever encountered, mainly because of Henry's policy of ordering at least one copy of everything, no matter how obscure, resulting in the shop having lots of interesting stuff that nobody else did. I instantly applied for the job. My Dad said that I was mad, as it was a dead-end job in a *"bloody record shop"*. My headmaster was even more scathing about me *"throwing my life away"* and tried everything to persuade me to stay on at school. Little did they know!

Ironically, I didn't get the job. Henry employed another young man, but after only a week, caught him stealing records and money from the till so sacked him on the spot. What happened next is one of my famous stories. I was helping my dad in the garden with his vegetable patch on a Sunday afternoon. Our house was on the corner of Norwich Road and Wood Mill Lane, high on a hill and I could see over the fence to the passing traffic below. I noticed this rather large posh Humber Hawk pull up and although I had never seen Henry's car in my life, a sixth sense told me that it was him. I was out of our front gate and outside his car before he'd even got out of the vehicle. He'd come to offer me the job. It was obviously meant to be and the rest - as we say - is history....

I wanted to start immediately but the bureaucracy and red tape at Taunton's Grammar wouldn't let me leave until the end of that term. I could have just walked out, but would have missed out on my leaving certificate, as well as upsetting my parents. I therefore started working as a Saturday assistant on 7th June 1969, two weeks before my sixteenth birthday, launching my career in the music industry. Under Henry's ownership, Pete Batt was still the Manager with Glyn Court, younger brother of old hand, Ken Court helping out as an occasional assistant.

The way that the staffing was structured saw Henry spending a lot of time doing the books (accounts payable and receivable), placing orders, receiving and checking them off. Henry mainly covered all the administration side plus particularly looking after the classical and easy listening customers. Pete did the electrical repair work, leaving it largely to me to look after the pop customers, and others with alternative eclectic musical tastes.

As a result of this, I very quickly established not only a great rapport with our regular customers, but very quickly worked out what was in demand, thus knowing exactly what we should be stocking and in what quantity. Henry did all of the ordering with the record company reps. Then on one fateful day, a record came out that completely changed my role in the shop. In September that year, the Philips rep, a Mr. George Page came in, to pre-sale the following month's (October) new releases. Amongst the many record labels that Philips distributed at the time was Island Records, the label formed by the very same Chris Blackwell that had released Millie's 'My Boy Lollipop' five years earlier.

Amongst the new releases was the debut LP by a new band called King Crimson entitled 'In the Court Of The Crimson King'. I of course knew that, not only, were most of the members of King Crimson local musicians, Robert Fripp, Mike Giles and Greg Lake having played locally in numerous Bournemouth bands since the early 60s, but that the band had made several live appearances on radio shows like John Peel's Top Gear showcasing the songs from their forthcoming LP.

The demand for it was enormous! As I'd spent most of the time in the shop serving customers on my own and hearing their enquiries first-hand, I knew how many times that we'd been asked for this LP. Henry, as I said earlier, had a policy of ordering at least one of everything, especially if it was only a new band, so after George had done his hard sell on King Crimson, Henry said that he would have *"just the one please"*.

The ground-breaking album cover was the creation of a young art student Barry Godber who had been given a demo tape of the disc which blew him away. The image remains one of the most iconic ever, as part of the new 'progressive rock' style – some found it 'disturbing' whilst most simply said it captured the music.

In the Court Of The Crimson King-album cover

I was completely amazed and immediately blurted out: *"We'll need at least a hundred of that - it's in huge demand!"*. *"A hundred.. a hundred??"* Henry exclaimed, *"I only order a hundred or more of the Beatles and The Rolling Stones!"* A discussion then ensued with George supporting my argument, and after some quick negotiation by Henry to ensure that he could get the record on a sale or return basis, he capitulated. *"Okay, lad, I'll give you a chance. I'll order fifty"*. This was in the days when newly issued LPs were released on Fridays, ready for the weekend trade. Our fifty copies of 'In the Court of The Crimson King' came in on the Friday and sold out by 3 o'clock on Saturday afternoon!

If we'd have ordered a hundred, we may have had enough stock to last until Tuesday when we would have got another delivery, having placed a further order on Monday morning. The LP entered the national Top Thirty LP chart at No.13 on 25th October, reaching No.4 by 8th November, continuing to sell well, right through Christmas. After learning from that experience, Henry decided to let me to do all of the ordering, so at the tender age of sixteen, I became the official buyer for Henry's Records! Precocious or what?

If the mid-Sixties had been watershed years with the new kinds of music evolving, the later years served only to expand horizons even more so with the advent of new creative genres such as the newly-named 'Progressive Rock' with not only King Crimson plus the likes of Pink Floyd, the Moody Blues, Family, Jethro Tull and Colosseum. The British Blues Boom was riding high with John Mayall, Fleetwood Mac, Free and Ten Years After, not forgetting the 'Folk Rock' arena led by Fairport Convention, Pentangle along with the crossover Byrds with their 'jingle jangle' Dylan covers.

'Country Rock' also ushered in, led by the likes of the Flying Burrito Brothers, with the latest Bob Dylan's 'Nashville Skyline' being a departure from his previous recordings following on from his original folk roots and controversial 'electric' change of direction.

Jazz Fusion led by Miles Davis was another minority style of music that was gaining in popularity, but the biggest leaps were heralded by the emergence of Classic Heavy Rock thanks to Led Zeppelin, Black Sabbath, Deep Purple et al. The other new wave came across from the USA headed by the brass rock style of Chicago and Blood, Sweat and Tears, not forgetting our own Portsmouth - based Heaven who appeared on the first two Isle of Wight Festivals in 1969 and 1970, headlined by Bob Dylan and Jimi Hendrix respectively. Santana gave us the new Latino Rock sounds, with Creedence Clearwater Revival's own 'swamp rock' lighting up the ever-changing charts.

Singer/songwriters were gradually beginning to emerge, seeing the likes of James Taylor, Carole King Joni Mitchell and Leonard Cohen heading the solo catalogues along with the 'hippy' influenced Crosby, Stills, Nash and Young who could really be labelled as the first 'Supergroup'

An early 'punk' style was emerging with the controversial Iggy Pop and The Stooges, and Velvet Underground (with Lou Reed) attracting a more rebellious section of youth, sowing the seeds of the late Seventies' feelings of disenchantment with music, mixed with political unrest. However, the three biggest British bands (Beatles, Stones, Who) were still riding high over everybody else as the end of that decade with 'Abbey Road, Let It Bleed and Tommy'.

Xmas 1969 – Echo adverts

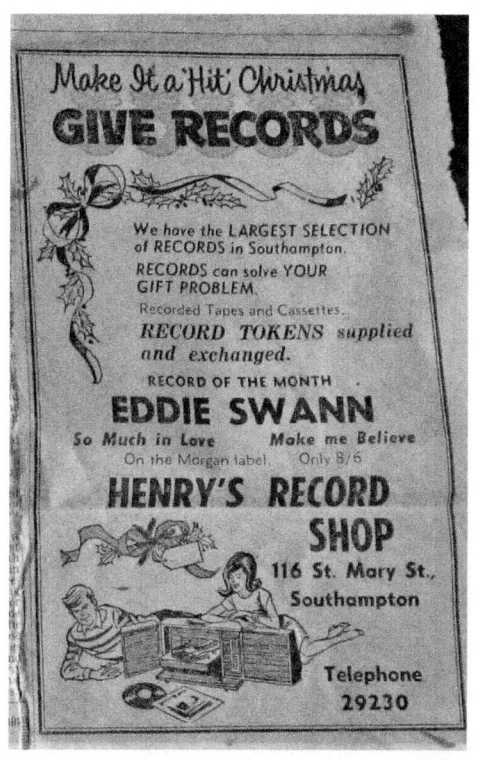

Over the next year with me buying in the right quantities of stock to meet demand, the sales turnover of records in the store quadrupled. Henry realized that he needed to focus more on recorded music, so gradually phased out the peripheral businesses of musical instruments, sheet music etc. Electrical goods still played a minor role but Pete Batt, realizing that the writing was on the wall, jumped ship to Gibbs Electronics in Shirley High St and our team was expanded to four with members Glen Clothier, to handle the odd electrical repairs that were still needed and Malcolm Jenks to help me with record sales. The four of us worked well during the next couple of years, as Henry's Records maintained its position as the best place for miles around, with many customers travelling long distances to browse through the record bins as well as 'talking shop' with us all.

Glen Clothier

As the wider breeds of music evolved, each of the major record companies created specialist labels to release this new music. EMI formed Harvest records, Philips created Vertigo, Decca launched Nova, Pye released on Dawn Records, with RCA having Neon. There were several new specialist labels such as Blue Horizon, owned by Mike Vernon for British blues. Chrysalis evolved from the booking agency of the same name, plus the Marmalade label instigated by former Cream and Yardbirds' manager, Giorgio Gomelsky. Transatlantic Records concentrated on folk, with Frank Zappa's output channelled by his Straight label. The Beatles had already launched their own Apple label, followed by Immediate Records, under Rolling Stones' manager, Andrew Loog Oldham and of course, Island Records who were still a major independent success.

Another initiative of mine was to start importing records from other countries, particularly the U.S.A. as peoples' tastes were becoming more esoteric and demanding, plus many hard to find and exciting new bands were emerging overseas. Their own parent record companies in the U.K. were often reluctant to release their material here in the UK, until it had become tried and tested. My idea certainly paid off, as the sales figures proved a success, along with boosting our profile and customer satisfaction.

John   Henry   Glen - 1970 team

We started specializing in importing U.S 45s to cater for the growing disco market. Some of the specialist importers that we dealt with included Stage One, Global Records, Vixen & Continental Record Distributors. Many of these rare recordings are now very collectable with high prices on auction sites. Around this time, we started coining one of our famous slogans *"You'll Get It At Henry's"* because if a record was only available in one country in the world and you were prepared to pay the price, we'd order it for you. Disco was another very important part of the business and growing significantly. The shop was the first choice for most of the area's top disc jockeys, amongst them being Johnny Dymond (Royal Pier) Arthur Sheriff (Top Rank Suite) Carole Hamilton, (Adam and Eve club). Others included Simon Peterson, Jon Ferris and Joe Craen, (Concorde Club) plus several more from the Avenue Artistes agency, such as Bob Deene, Tommy Kaye, Mike Windsor, Dave Carson, Geoff Knight and Chris Golden. At the shop's peak, we were supplying about ninety different DJs!

As the new releases came out on Fridays, many of the 'jocks' would try and get in early on that day, sometimes two or three of them together. I would have a pile of all of the new releases on the counter, one of each, letting them take the ones that they wanted to listen to. They then took their selections to the end of the shop, placing the discs on a standalone record player, to choose which discs would suit their particular audiences in the diverse venues. These guys (and girl) really knew their stuff, as any former club-goer would tell you to this day, with the DJs keeping the dance floors packed in between the live bands, thus complementing each other on great nights out. I dedicate the next small chapter to these wonderful people, many of whom are still 'spinning the platters' to this day, as well as remaining good mates. Tinged with sadness as we have all lost so many 'jocks', musicians and customers whose paths we all crossed during those never to be forgotten years.

The following short chapter shows just a few of the many DJs that kept the dance floors packed, adapting to the mood of the crowd with ever changing music for all tastes.

CHAPTER 6. THE 'JOCKS'
SOME OF THE MANY POPULAR D.J.s

Many of the local disc jockeys were managed by Avenue Artistes Ltd, originally founded in the late Fifties by impresario Len Canham who ran the Royal Pier Pavilion Ballroom for many years. Most of them had an extensive collection of vinyl records that had to be lugged around in heavy boxes when performing mobile shows on the road. Very different from today when thousands of tracks are stored on tiny memory sticks to be played via a laptop or other digital outlets.

I keep in regular contact with several of these pals, many of whom have still retained their precious singles and albums. Some stored in lofts but others on shelves in spare rooms, carefully catalogued thus enabling selections to be placed on a new high-tech turntable. Fed through expensive sound systems to be enjoyed in their original recording format – nothing beats it!

Like me, Chris Golden emigrated to another beautiful country albeit a bit closer to the UK. Another very popular jock who was the resident DJ at many top venues including the Royal Pier and other clubs and dance halls around Southampton.

He left the shores to settle in Canada, where he held a prestigious position in charge of the Winnipeg Transport system, alongside his music gigs. Chris has hosted several radio shows in the city so can easily be found by internet searches as and when he moves around. He has also made the trip back to Southampton on several occasions, visiting family and friends as well as arranging the dates to coincide with David St John's annual 'Back to the Sixties' reunion shows since 2008. Chris has stepped back in the DJ booth, rubbing shoulders with his former fellow jocks to play the classic hits in between the live groups – just as they all did back in the Glory Days!

The name of Johnny Dymond is probably the most remembered name from the time that he moved down from Grimsby to take up the residency at the Royal Pier, working in partnership with Len Canham.

This when Mecca took over the ballroom with its new décor that stirs the memories of the potted palm trees around the sides of the dance floor lit by thousands of reflections from the giant disco mirror ball on the ceiling.

Labelled 'Mr Romance' with Johnny spinning the platters as the various groups took their breaks or simply filled the whole evening on his own, leading to the last few slow dances for the 'smoochers' to get closer. This led to many new relationships and marriages across these years, so a big thanks to JD as we call him. John was also promoted by Avenue Artistes, in addition to writing his brilliant record reviews in 'The Southern Entertainer'. This in-house magazine only last for three issues from December 1963, recently published by David St John via his Amazon Book page, giving a great look back at that exciting time as Beatlemania was breaking out. He is also responsible for sharing many photos on DSJ's website across several pages so well worth a look. Johnny moved out to Southern Spain following his long career, but still retaining strong links with his adopted hometown.

Dave Carson was another successful DJ, sadly no longer with us having passed away at a young age.

D.C. spent many years as a mobile jock plus residencies in addition to his time spent on Radio Victory broadcasting from Portsmouth across the South, gaining a wide following. His family has a nice Facebook Tribute page that keeps his memory alive. Dave also played for the Avenue Artistes football team, leading to loads of laughs on and off the pitch with the antics of all concerned as you might imagine!

Steve Davies (below) was another regular fixture on the Hampshire scene for many years and a regular customer of ours, enjoying great chats about the music on his visits to the shop.

A very special part of the scene was the gorgeous Carole Hamilton, best known for her residency at the Adam & Eve Club in Spa Road, just behind the old Echo offices on Above Bar. The old site was demolished to make way for the new Westquay shopping centre that dominates the city centre. She also spun records at Fridays club on London Road, being best known for her top class selections of Soul and Tamla Motown hits. In recent years Carole has hosted A&E Reunion Nights that see the former dancers take to the floor yet again in amongst the younger types that just love a taste of what it was all about in their parents' – or grandparents' day!

One of her regular venues is back at the Concorde Club so why not check out the events page to see as and when she hits the decks again? There were very few female DJs or even group members during the Sixties/Seventies, so the likes of Carole had several male followers as you can surmise. One of her many publicity photos shows why….

"Just come across your website and it brought back some very happy memories, especially regarding the Adam & Eve nightclub and Henry's Records. I was actually the DJ on the very last night at the Adam and Eve and it came as quite a shock when the woman who owned it called us all together at the end of the night to say it was closing. We had a wonderful Sunday afternoon at her house finishing off the booze a week or so later but I've always wondered what happened to all the records! My memories of Henry's Records are also quite vivid as they tried to prise me away from HMV where I worked in the store in the Bargate at

that time. I used to get on very well with John Clare, both as a customer and friend and every so often I would buy the records for the A&E from there as well.

I went on to work for HMV in various positions for 30 years and travelled the world with them but it all started in Southampton in the heady days of 1972 so I've got many memories of vinyl, 8 tracks, open reel tapes, cassettes, CDs etc. Thanks for bringing it all back!"

Joe Craen remains another good mate from the early days as we often reminisce about our respective lives. He now lives in Staffordshire but often returns to the South for family visits plus guest appearances at the Concorde Club where he could be found in his earlier times on the circuit.

Like many of his peers, Joe has managed to keep thousands of old records and memorabilia from his own past, leading us into many a deep conversation on the phone. We talk for hours about the more obscure releases that cropped up in between the more popular chart music – he has an amazing knowledge and recall so we often bounce facts off each other as self-confessed 'vinyl junkies' Much better than hard drugs. A favourite pic of us two below.

Simon Peterson – another familiar face around the many dance halls, clubs and venues across the South.

Likewise – Arthur Sheriff who many will remember from his stints at the Top Rank Suite, a futuristic banqueting suite that hosted top chart names and top class resident bands. It was built on the site of the old Stadium owned by Charlie Knott, staging greyhound racing, speedway, banger racing and the like. Part of the Top Rank area that had the Ice Rink and Tenpin Bowling Alley across the way.

This rare photo shows a bearded Arthur Sheriff blowing a kiss at one of the Top Rank Suite management team! Pictured by the stairs leading to the balcony area.

The 1977 hit of 'Uptown Top Ranking' by Althea and Donna neatly summed up the fun-filled nights out at this classic venue. Its revolving stage allowed the various cabaret acts and groups to set their equipment in readiness for their spots as the DJs out front kept the dance floor packed.

The final two photos in this chapter feature another couple of disc jockeys, the first being a nice memory of Tommy Kaye's smile that lit up many a room. Yet another mate who passed away at a relatively young age after many successful years in the business. I could probably fill another book, highlighting so many more of these showmen (and women) but I'm glad to have included just a few of them in these pages.

Tommy Kaye, followed by a hairy Steve Quinn in a classic setting that will strike many a chord. Not sure which club or pub but maybe this was a resident set-up on a small stage?

    I guess that some reader will recognise the décor, probably taken during the Seventies as per Steve's look of that time? Nice to look back at the 'vintage' equipment with home-made front screens shielding the twin decks. Plus a shelf full of the 45s ready for the rest of the night – a stark contrast to our high-tech 21st Century DJ profiles with high output sound system and start of the art lighting rigs that take much more time to set up!

CHAPTER 7. THE SEVENTIES - CHANGES

Another lucrative and very important part of the business was supplying the local Juke Box companies. They would buy multiple copies of five or six different records from the Top 40 each week to put on their juke boxes, resulting in orders of over 500 records per company. We offered an additional service to these companies, with the use of a special piece of equipment known in the business as a 'Dinking Machine'. This labour-saving device quickly popped the centres out of 45s creating the larger hole, making them ready to go on to the American juke box turntables. We were the only shop in town that had this facility at that time, as well as stocking the small plastic inserts (known as 'spiders'), that were bought by customers who needed them to slot back into the used records, sold out of the second-hand boxes in our own shop and other outlets.

Our main juke box company customers were Liberty Coin, run by American Herbie Katz at the bottom of St Mary Street, along with Revis Automatics on the corner of Hill Lane and Commercial Road, owned by Reg Bicknell. Along with his wife Leigh, owning the famous Checkpoint Café by the Bargate, as well as the legendary Adam & Eve Club. Others were Auto-Play and Display-Matics, all of these companies keeping the balance sheets healthy for many years. Other constant visitors to the shop were the various representatives of the record companies. With some larger companies such as CBS, Pye and RCA, the rep was a van salesman, arriving every week with his vehicle full of records. We simply handed him an order which was then selected from his mobile stock outside on the road, then delivered straight away. Because of the well-known friendliness of the Henry's Records staff, these reps would usually try and arrive around mid-day, to have a break in our back room. It wasn't uncommon to find three or four of these chaps at any given lunch time eating fish and chips at the back of the shop!

Another great tradition if they couldn't make lunch time was to come a bit earlier in the day to enjoy 'Enry's Elevenses', a mid-morning tea-break, which usually included a red-hot home baked lardy cake straight from the oven, dripping with treacle from Biglands Bakery on the corner of St Mary and Ascupart Street. The other bigger record companies like EMI, Decca, Philips and Polydor had reps that came every month to pre-sale next month's releases. Any weekly orders that we required had to be phoned through for delivery the next day, if you got the order in before 10 o'clock. As the store closed for half-day trading on Wednesdays at 1 o'clock, it soon became another tradition for these reps to turn up on Wednesday lunch time, when we would retire to the pub across the road, the Kingsland Tavern, in order do our business over a liquid lunch! Of course, the reps still had to carry on the rest of their days work afterwards, with some being better at being careful about their alcoholic intake than others!

Then there were the Trade Nights, when record companies invited the dealers to special evening functions with food and drink to launch some special new act or record label, presumably in the hope that we would consume enough alcohol to give them some ridiculously large opening order (well that's my theory anyway!). They were always really good nights. Some that I vividly remember were an Island Records night to launch new act, Emerson, Lake and Palmer, a Decca night to launch the Moody Blues own label, Threshold and a Pye Records night to showcase their new progressive label, Dawn. This shows Malcolm Jenks, me, Angela Fearne, Peter Gifford, Eric Fearne and Henry. Eric owned the well-known Jack Hobbs Records in Eastleigh – formerly the bicycle shop run by Angela's father. Eric phoned Henry every Friday for topping up his stocks for the Saturday trade as well being best pals. Henry dropped the order off on his way home.

Around this time, we also had a window promotion for local acts – Tex Roberg and Bob Pearce as seen here.

In 1971, the shop decided to update their bag for customers and the famous record rising out of the heap design was created. The design was supposed to symbolize the *"You'll Get It At Henry's"* motto by depicting that, out of all the records available (at the bottom of the bag), we can raise up that special one that you are looking for! All very arty and profound for its time. Originally, we had a paper version in purple and orange, but then as business grew, the profits allowed us to afford more money, so we had a very posh plastic version in blue & gold.

Other memorable features of the store were the listening booths where customers could listen to records played back from the desk.
As we were by now ordering a lot of big selling LPs in the hundreds, extra storage space was needed. The empty spaces above the booths were soon used to stack two hundred copies of the latest Elton John album alongside another two hundred of Rod Stewart's release. This, in addition to many more LPs spread across the length of the booths, made out of plywood.

One memorable day still makes me smile as I was extolling the merits of the opening track of the new Led Zeppelin LP, 'Immigrant Song' to one of our regular customers. *"Just listen to the bass on this"* I exclaimed, as I cranked up both the bass and volume to one of the turntables that supplied music to his listening cubicle. The whole shop shook, as did the booths which all vibrated, resulting in a few thousand stacked LPs dislodged to fall all over the shop floor. Henry was not amused as you can imagine, but luckily none were damaged, so we just laughed it off, as I spent the next hour picking them all up, to carefully re-stack them! The volume at which I played records in the store, often had to compete with the noisy hammering and drilling emanating from Glen in the workshop at the back. Not only did he repair electrical goods, but also put together record cabinets and TV units – a real handy man.

1972 saw two major challenges to the business. First of all, Edward Heath's Conservative government introduced V.A.T. (Value Added Tax) on everything at the rate of 10%. This meant that every single item in the store had to be re-priced to display the increase - a massive job which saw us working over the course of a Saturday and Sunday night to complete. This obviously didn't help business, as everything was now more expensive to buy, although the general public begrudgingly got used to it, with things settling down after a short while. Fortunately, our faithful customers shrugged it all off, not allowing any government to curtail their spending habits on one of their main pleasures in life.

The other (bigger) problem that happened in that same year saw EMI opening their own chain of record shops, under the name of HMV Records (the old His Master's Voice). Their new outlet started to trade near the old Bargate in Southampton's city centre – a prime location for all main shops. Overnight, we had to compete with a larger shop owned by a record company, whose buying power was naturally far greater than our own. On top of that, Heath had abolished RPM - the 'retail price maintenance' a few years earlier, in order to encourage competition, but this naturally led to the inevitable price-cutting wars on the High Street.

This had a major impact on the smaller family-owned businesses such as ours, but we managed to weather the storm in spite of the threat. Ironically, one of our regular customers was Paul Brixey – resident DJ at the Adam and Eve nightclub, who landed himself a job at the new HMV. Starting out as a sales assistant, then very quickly working himself up the ladder to Store Manager, a couple of years later.

1973 ushered in the beginnings of computerization, so when we phoned orders through to the record companies on a Monday morning, the girls on the end of the phone were no longer writing down the record catalogue numbers by hand. Instead, they were now inputting the information into a computer, with some operatives making mistakes by using the new technology. Of course, we all know that computers are only as good as the person entering the data. This led to us receiving loads of wrong records, as their staff had not typed in the correct numbers, causing Henry's frustration and extra time-consuming duties, as he had to re-package the discs. He then had to send them back, requesting credit for the unwanted stock, as well as writing letters to the record companies' head office, to explain and complain.

Another major change came in 1973, as we finally decided to give up selling electrical items due to the emerging continual domination of the market by large electrical chain stores such as Curry's and Dixons, not being able to compete in the face of this competition. On top of this, recorded music was now a major growing business helped mainly by the fact that every album, as they now began to be called, was released in three different formats, LPs, cassette tapes and 8 track cartridges for the growing portable audio and in-car audio markets.

Pink Floyd's 'Dark Side of The Moon' was one of the earliest albums to be released simultaneously in these three formats, Other early Seventies releases saw several more groundbreaking, blockbusting albums that flew out of the shop, including these classic releases that are still relevant to this day. Sticky Fingers/ Rolling Stones, Who's Next/The Who, Imagine/John Lennon, Four Symbols/Led Zeppelin, Tapestry/Carole King, Every Picture Tells a Story/Rod Stewart, L.A. Woman/The Doors, What's Going On/Marvin Gaye, Layla/Eric Clapton, All Things Must Pass/George Harrison, Surf's Up/The Beach Boys, Ziggy Stardust/David Bowie, Talking Book/Stevie Wonder, Roxy Music's debut album, Close to the

Edge/Yes, Tranformer/Lou Reed, American Pie/Don McLean, Band on the Run/Wings – all amongst so many more amazing albums that I had the privilege of playing as soon as they arrived, ahead of the general public.

In amongst the giant record companies, a new name cropped up who would eventually become one of the biggest corporate names in the UK. Ex-public schoolboy Richard Branson, despite being dyslexic, had shown entrepreneurial skills in his late teens by launching 'The Student' magazine which made him a considerable sum that helped to kick start his next enterprise. The publication was the perfect vehicle to advertise his new mail order record business, although he carried very little stock, choosing to get the orders first, then buy in loads of imported records. Germany was a major source, due to the new British interest in 'Kraut Rock', but not widely available in this country. He took out full page listings in the NME, again not actually stocking the actual discs until receiving the orders, then quickly getting them over from across the Channel. His first 'office' was a dingy basement in the now-fashionable Connaught Square, just off Marble Arch in London's West End. Within a short time, he managed to rent a small shop in nearby Oxford Street, his first major steps to becoming a billionaire.

He was able to afford a mansion in Oxfordshire, with its own recording studio – The Manor, leading to the release of 'Tubular Bells' by Mike Oldfield on Branson's new Virgin Label. The rest is history as we know. Little did we realise that Virgin, amongst others, would be a later nemesis of small independent records shops including Henry's.

After some three years, Glen Clothier left in 1973, with Malcolm Jenks remaining until 1975. Other junior assistants came and went, including Peter Beaton, Peter Simmons, Tim Foad and Alan Wooller. In 1974, due to business having now expanded beyond the realms of our expectations, due partly to my product knowledge and customer service skills, Henry chose to make me his junior partner. At the same time, he decided to make the business a limited company, thereby protecting our liabilities if anything went wrong. We became Henry's

Records Ltd and, at the tender age of twenty one, I became Managing Director! Henry became Chairman, his long-standing friend, accountant and financial adviser, Andrew Ramage-Gibson became secretary, with Henry's mother Rose becoming a fourth 'sleeping partner'. It was a good move on Henry's part to make me a shareholder, as it only increased my commitment and determination to make the business more and more successful. Our 1969-1974 staff photo shows me, Peter Batt, Glen Clothier, Henry, Malcolm Jenks and Tim Foad- a great team.

The personal appearances continued with Mick Jagger's young brother Chris Jagger attempting to make a dent in the business, in the footsteps of his older brother. GM Records, a subsidiary of Phillips, had invested a great deal of money in the young wannabe, but he failed to make any impact on the charts, so simply 'faded away' – a nod to an early Stones hit.

He was followed by George McCrae in 1974, following up his previous No. 1 smash 'Rock Your Baby' with 'I Can't Leave You Alone' but this never took off in the same way. Liverpool's The Real Thing hit the no. 1 spot in 1976 with 'You to Me Are Everything' attracting big crowds when they called by to promote their follow-up releases. In the words of Bob Dylan, the times were 'a changing' with the new Labour Party, under Harold Wilson, now in charge of a problem-laden country. The Seventies was a time of recession, wage restraints, political unrest with high unemployment figures, leading to young people in England finding it more difficult to get a job.

We not only had much more staunch opposition from the likes of HMV, on top of wage restraints, major strikes plus an international recession. A revolution was waiting to take place. not only in the country at large, but also in the music industry, as the record buying public grew more and more tired of long rambling solos from the self-indulgent progressive rock bands. There was a degree of snobbery amongst some of these outfits as they looked down their smug noses at commercial music. The late Seventies witnessed the emergence of the young unemployed wannabe musicians forming 'garage bands' under a new label of Punk Music. Partly due to expressing their anger and dissatisfaction with the world, as well as sticking two fingers up to the Establishment. The Sex Pistols and others led the way in a major shake-up within the young record buying public – disaffected youth up against the mainstream music fans.

The 45-rpm single, which had taken a back seat to the creative, arty concept albums put out by the more adventurous, classically trained and forward-thinking rock improvisers, was about to enjoy a resurgence almost in equal to the Beat Boom Sixties. Not only due to the impending punk rock explosion, but because of the disco boom driven by another new development. The 12-inch single with extended remix versions of current disco hits, came into vogue, offering more than the standard playing time of the 45 singles plus extra tracks with different arrangements etc.

Around this time, I started adding other strings to my bow when I was invited by my good friend, Joe Craen to take over as his DJ partner from Simon Peterson at the prestigious Concorde Club in Stoneham Lane. This venue first saw the light of day back in 1957, when a young jazz musician, Cole Mathieson set up his own small club in the back room of the Bassett Hotel on Burgess Road , near the top of the Common. It hosted a folk club and, inspired by the new wave of R&B music during the early Sixties, featured the early Manfred Mann as the resident house band. The likes of Rod Stewart, Robert Plant, Elton John, Eric Clapton and many more future 'names' trod the boards until reaching global fame and fortune within a short time. The Concorde moved to the larger premises in the early Seventies, going from strength to strength ever since. Joe Craen was one of our main customers, thus able to purchase the right records for a very discerning audience at this venue who were not necessarily locked into chart music of the time.

This was to be the beginning of my secondary 'career' in broadcasting, enjoying the buzz of the club, as we played some great new music to keep the dance floor packed for hours. The feedback was very humbling as well as being paid to spin the discs at a much higher volume, recalling my previous escapade in Henry's shop, when Led Zeppelin caused a cascade to fall from the top of the record booths!

The name of Bob Pearce is revered across the British Blues scene, with a long history of fronting several changes of his Blues Band from the early Sixties, following on from his 1964 Footprints r&b group. His superb vocals, guitar and harmonica skills have been preserved on many albums, including the late 70s release of 'Colour Blind' on the Hampshire-based Forest Tracks label. Once again, we cleared our window to market this latest offering, leading to very high sales amongst his massive fan base. Bob's line-up of his Blues band went through many changes across several years, including several top-rated musicians. They also supported many visiting USA blues stars on their visits to the UK, often by request as their reputation was well established in many overseas countries.

The following photos show the promotional window display plus a signed photo of the band in action.

Left to right : Joz Jones, Bob Pearce, Pete Harris, Henry Wright, John Livermore Carl Leyland.

"To Henry's Records with many best wishes. The shop with the Blues" Bob Pearce

Bob remains a great pal to these days, in addition to being my Best Man when getting married. His other skills were often used when designing posters and newspaper adverts, including this example.

One of the other perks of being in the record industry was that, at any time that any major act toured, that you were a fan of, all you had to do was ask your friendly rep if they had any free tickets for local performances. Invariably, if you'd looked after them and made a good job of promoting their product, they would be very obliging in giving you a couple of tickets. These were often in prestigious seats in the middle of the front row, or in a box overlooking the stage. The list of top name artists that I saw during the Seventies reads like a Who's Who of the music industry.

This Hall of Fame included Paul McCartney/Wings, David Bowie and The Spiders from Mars, Bob Marley and the Wailers, Bob Dylan, The Beach Boys, Van Morrison, Abba, Eric Clapton, Fleetwood Mac, Genesis, Cliff Richard, Marvin Gaye, Roxy Music, Dire Straits, Kate Bush, Meatloaf, Ry Cooder, The Rolling Stones, Rod Stewart and The Faces, Jethro Tull, Joni Mitchell, The Eagles, Stevie Wonder and Thin Lizzy, all of which never cost me a cent! Sometimes they were in my hometown of Southampton, or just twenty odd miles away in Bournemouth or Portsmouth. Often, they were in London and I probably travelled to London two or three times a month to catch a show.

The real coup de grace for me was the British debut of one Bruce Springsteen and The E Street Band at Hammersmith Odeon. I had discovered Bruce by importing his first three albums via Stage One Records, way before CBS/UK had had any plans to release him in the UK. It was only after his much heralded third album 'Born to Run' that they finally saw the light. At that time, CBS had set up their own promotional division, with local boys Alvin Jordan and Richard Comben being part of that team. They were therefore good contacts of mine and I had been making big noises about 'The Boss' for over a year.

They were presented with four precious tickets, for the debut concert, including invites to the after-concert drinks and nibbles, two of them being for themselves, with me being the lucky recipient of one of the remaining two. The other lucky fellow was Radio Solent presenter, Gethyn Jones. We all travelled up in a limo, with seats in the circle overlooking the left side of the stage. Needless to say, the concert was amazing and the after-concert event packed with other CBS recording acts such as Ian Hunter, Roger Waters of Pink Floyd (they recorded for CBS in the U.S) and of all people, Andy Williams!

The closest that I could get to Bruce though was about five metres, as he was continually surrounded by people, but still, it is my most famous encounter and a lasting memory. As a result of that night out and my meeting with Gethyn Jones, I was then invited to join his team on the cult BBC Radio Solent show 'Solent Rock' with another colourful local personality called Oliver Gray. It was a great experience, as we played records, then talked about them in between, as opposed to many presenters who simply had to follow the radio station's play-list, with little or no background information that the listeners wanted.

CHAPTER EIGHT: 21ST ANNIVERSARY

The long hot 1976 saw a completely new team of staff at Henry's. Malcolm Jenks had left after 3 years' service, replaced by Paul Vincent, poached from HMV, albeit at the recommendation of HMV's then-manager, Paul Brixey. 'Vince' as Paul Vincent was affectionately known had been looking for a full-time position which HMV couldn't offer. Our new team was completed by junior assistant, Steve Crimble. In May 1976, due mainly to the ever increasing aggressive competition from the chain stores, the other major long-serving independent shop in town, Francis Records decided to close its doors. Owner John Francis' interview for the Southern Evening Echo on May 24 said it all. *"With everyone selling records except Mothercare and Mac Fisheries, the business has been running at a loss for over a year, despite attracting regular customers over an area from Fareham to Bournemouth"*

Our own business still continued to grow, in spite of the increasing competition. Besides the many sales of disco singles both on 7 and 12 inch, there was a new wave of garage bands from the U.S. such as The Ramones, The Patti Smith Group and Talking Heads. The other real money spinner for Henry's was that we were selling countless amounts of all sorts of Reggae 45s on masses of different smaller independent record labels to supply the large demand coming from Southampton's Caribbean community. Many of these living in the nearby St Mary's Rd / Derby Rd / Newtown area just the other side of Six Dials roundabout, from the shop. Most of our supply came from independent distributor, Robbie Day, a former Radio Caroline DJ.

That same year of 1976 witnessed our long-term involvement with the Southern Evening Echo began. We were approached by journalist, Steve Clarke who had been asked to run a new music column called 'Off the Record'. He wanted us to provide him with a Top Ten singles and albums chart every weekend, with this relationship continuing throughout the next six years, with successive writers of the column including Gary Lovejoy, Bob Everitt and Tim Witcher. Steve started off the first edition column with a feature highlighting Henry's Records called 'A Day with Our Top Ten Men'. Naturally, during the next few years as my focus on local bands became more involved, I was very influential in convincing these journalists on who to focus on in their column.

1977 was a watershed year. First of all, on August 16th, an era ended with the tragic death of the King of Rock and Roll, Elvis Presley. In all my twenty years at Henry's Records, I have never witnessed record sales like it, in the wake of this momentous event. Fortunately for us, and this might sound mercenary, we had a policy of stocking all back catalogue albums of the giants of music like Elvis in big quantities. We were well stocked to meet the demand, especially as his record company, RCA very quickly ran out of a lot of the more popular titles. Within two weeks of his death, Elvis had nine posthumous albums in the Top 30. His latest album 'Moody Blue' at No. 1, the previous album 'Welcome to My World' at No 6, '40 Greatest Hits' at No 9, 'G.I Blues' at No 20, 'Elvis In Demand' at No. 22, 'Elvis Golden Records' at No. 23, 'Elvis Golden Records No. 2' at No. 24, 'The Sun Collection' at No. 25 and 'Blue Hawaii' at No. 26. A better showing in the album charts than he ever had in his heyday in the Fifties! The 'In Demand' album was another recent release, just prior his death, RCA producing a limited-edition giant poster of the album cover for record shops only, embossed in gold, to be used in window displays. We were one of the lucky record shops to have one, so I set up an incredible Elvis window display using this as a centre piece. One of my biggest regrets is that I never took a photo of that window display or kept the large poster.

Then on November 26th, almost heralding an 'out with the old - in with the new' scenario, EMI released the debut single by the Sex Pistols: 'Anarchy in the U.K'. A whole raft of other punk bands followed in their wake, resurrecting sales of 45s to unprecedented numbers, unknown since the Sixties. At the same time, a lot of independent ('indie') record labels sprung up led by Jake Riviera's Stiff Records featuring The Damned, Elvis Costello and the Attractions plus Ian Dury and The Blockheads. Others included Step Forward Records with Chelsea (who became Generation X), The Fall and Sham 69, Fast Records with The Gang of Four, The Dead Kennedys and Human League and of course the U.S. Sire label with the Ramones, Talking Heads, The Rezillos and The Undertones. The really big leader in the indie market was to come a year later with the formation of Rough Trade, who not only became a label in its own right but became a major distributor for all independent labels, as well as having its own retail shop in London.

The other major event of the year was that at the end of November, Henry's Records celebrated twenty one years in business with a big birthday bash held at the historic Dolphin Hotel in Below Bar, Southampton. Loads of record company people were invited past and present, as well as our loyal DJs (most of whom should have been working as it was a main Saturday night) and some regular customers. Fil Towers, National Sales Manager of Phonogram presented Henry with a gold disc and Bob Lewis, National Sales Manager of CBS, presented him with a silver disc to commemorate the event. We took out a full page in the Echo with editorial, in which most of the major record companies placed ads to pay for the great coverage.

We were presented with a copy Silver disc of 'Bridge Over Troubled Water' album sales as well as a Gold copy of the Welcome Home' Peters & Lee million seller.

It was certainly a night to remember, followed by placing these discs on the shop walls amongst many other awards gained over the previous years. Our faces show how proud we were of achieving this milestone.

Henry thanked all concerned for one of his best nights ever, followed by a group photograph of the many guests, then into a disco finale to end a memorable night.

We then decided in order to celebrate the landmark event that we would re-design our bag yet again, and in a fit of extreme vanity, Henry and I decided to have our pictures on the bag with the mandate 'Come to the Experts! The drawings were done by local blues musician Bob Pearce, who had become a good friend and whose daytime job was as a graphic artist. The photos that he used as the template for the drawings were taken by an old school friend of mine who was by now a professional photographer, Ainsley Adams - one of my greatest lifelong friends, who sadly died of cancer just a few years ago.

By 1978, the staff had changed briefly again with Paul Vincent being replaced by Arthur Richfield, former assistant at Sydney's Men's Outfitters across the road which had by now closed down. Two junior assistants came along in quick succession, Tony Fowler and Paul Joslin. However, after the 21st Anniversary, Henry started taking more and more of a back seat, leaving me to run more of the day-to-day business of the shop, so I needed a strong lieutenant. We then took on Pete Bentley who formerly ran the record department of Rumbelows department store in Eastleigh. He naturally had some buying experience, aided by another new face of Phil McCarthy, who reminded me of myself as a 16-year-old, himself already having a wide taste and knowledge of music. Pete's expertise was soul and disco, so naturally took over the personal service of our seventy odd disc jockey customers, in addition to overseeing the Top 40 singles, plus the juke box orders. Pete was given the job of buyer for all singles ordering except the punk/indie stuff, which was left to me along with the album and cassette ordering, 8 track cartridges now gradually becoming obsolete. This formidable team stayed together for the next four years until 1982 - not only the longest surviving outfit but easily the best overall in terms of music expertise. No other record shop - big or small could compete with the personal service that we offered across the years in business.

By 1979, I was still very busy with Henry's Records, on top of my continuing involvement with Radio Solent's 'Solent Rock' programme. The show was virtually split 50/50 with Gethyn Jones spinning the latest rock vinyl, plus Oliver Gray heavily promoting the local live band scene including his famous gig guide. My role initially was to feature an album of the week, play a couple of tracks, then talk about it in some depth. It became a perfect vehicle for me to plug the shop, much against the BBC's non advertising stance but Gethyn (good on him) always let them slip through.

I was heavily involved in the local music scene, regularly going out to local live gigs, two or three times a week. The nearest being The Joiners Arms, my local down the road in St Mary St, plus every Saturday night at The Onslow in Bevois Valley, the regular residency for several years for the various Bob Pearce Blues band line-ups. Other haunts like The Gryphon in Shirley and The Red Lion in Bitterne spring to mind amongst so many venues across the city.

Many of these same musicians were regular customers buying records from our shop in between popping by for a chat about the whole music scene in general. It was no surprise that I quickly became part of the local aspect of the show with Oliver, regularly inviting bands that I knew onto the show, to play their latest demo tapes and chat. It became inevitable that, in the spirit of the indie label scene, a lot of local bands self-funded and put out recordings of their own stuff. The only shop where you could exclusively buy these recordings was, of course, Henry's Records.

My first involvement was with the aforementioned Bob Pearce. He had originally put out a solo album on the little-known Welsh independent folk and blues label, Westwood Records in 1974 called 'Let's Get Drunk Again'. Guess where you could buy that? That's right *"You'll Get It At Henry's"*. Now, with his full blues band, he was making an album for Forest Tracks Records, the local folk and blues label co-owned by local folk singer Dave Williams, Echo reporter John Edgar Mann and Australian businessman, Gordon Mignot. The only two places that you could buy the album were direct from Forest Tracks, or at Henry's Records.

As I went to the Onslow every Saturday night, I started selling the album there and at every other Bob Pearce gig. The album became one of Henry's Records biggest selling albums of 1979, out-selling big-name heavyweights like Abba: 'The Album', Police: 'Regatta De Blanc' and Kate Bush: 'The Kick Inside', but not out-selling 'Saturday Night Fever', the massive phenomenon of the year as the disco boom exploded worldwide.

In 1979, I was invited to present a weekly show on Southampton University's own radio station, Radio Glen, hosting the weekly 'Night Rock' on Monday nights from 11-00 pm until 1 am, which became yet another perfect vehicle for plugging Henry's Records. The show featured a variety of all music genres but having a very strong leaning towards the indie music scene which was of course very popular with the students. Other strings to my bow included finally fulfilling my schoolboy fantasy of becoming a musical journalist by writing regular record reviews and live gig reviews for two local publications, 'Stick It in Your Ear' and 'Due South'. The next two photos show Gethyn on Radio Solent plus my own slot on Radio Glen where I had free rein to play my favourite music as well as being appreciated by the students as our tastes matched each other.

My own show on Radio Glen at Southampton University.

This wonderful dual life between the record shop, radio and my outings to pubs and clubs were sowing the seeds of an idea that had been buzzing in my head for some while. The national music press naturally highlighted the big names of the day, whilst scant attention was paid to the thousands of 'unknown' acts who made great music, especially those I got to know on my own patch. Around this time I started to write up my notes that led to another facet of my life.

Another huge selling local release on Forest Tracks was the Gutta Percha and The Balladeers' novelty single of 'The Woolston Ferry'. Southampton City Council had built the new impressive Itchen Bridge spanning the river, linking Woolston with the city, opened in 1977, but sadly with the loss of the former chain-driven Floating Bridges, much missed by those who had travelled across over many years on those wonderful ferries. 'Gutta Percha' (aka local folk singer Mike Sadler) decided to write and record a commemorative song.

As his group included Dave Williams on guitar and accordion, it was no surprise, that they should release it on Forest Tracks, Dave being a director! Another Henry's exclusive, the sales absolutely blew us away, selling over a thousand copies, remaining at no.1 in the 'Henry's Top Ten Chart' published in the Echo for weeks on end. It was even outselling the Beatles back catalogue which had provided a steady income for record shops everywhere.

The Balladeers were one of many popular acts, performing in folk clubs all over the South, with many of their own followers being good customers as we stocked a wide selection of that genre, as well as being able to cater for any unusual requests for obscure recordings. This all enhanced our 'specialist' profile, of which we were very proud plus giving us all a chance to hear a wide spectrum of music played while we worked.

This historic recording can be found on YouTube with lyrics, plus old movie footage of the much-missed 'Floaties' as we called these wonderful ferries. Many late passengers got a soaking when running for the ferry in an effort to jump onto the departing ramp as it left the hard, but ending up in the water. Others will recall missing the last crossing of the night – usually midnight on either side. The local buses were then due to make their own final journeys a few minutes after the last ferries had departed, but occasionally left a bit early – maybe for laughs? The angry late night revellers then faced a few miles of walking north to cross the Northam Bridge or share a taxi if being able to afford it.

The 1978 team was the best we ever had with Pete Bentley and Phil McCarthy as shown above and below.

CHAPTER 9.. THE EIGHTIES - VINYL TAKES A DIP

The Eighties rolled in, with more landmark events on the way, including the awful loss of John Lennon on the 8th December 1980, thanks to a deranged music fan in New York. A revolutionary turning point came along in January 1983, with the launch of the compact disc, jointly developed by Sony in Japan and Phillips in Holland. The optical disc, which was read by a laser, rather than the gramophone record which needed to be tracked by a diamond stylus, was recorded digitally, rather than the old analogue system employed by earlier records. This meant that the sound quality was unbelievably better, in fact fairly close to the original sound, as recorded and intended in the studio, by the engineer in charge of the recording session that produced that original album.

Furthermore, because compact discs or CDs as they became known, were read by a laser, it meant that the discs, which were really transparent and coated with a silver lacquer, had no defects in the performance of the disc, no matter how scratched or marked they became, i.e. no more jumping, sticking or surface noise, as the laser just fired through the scratched silver surface to read the digitally encoded information underneath. Unlike the old vinyl, they could be played thousands of times with no loss of quality, apart from any dirt or heavy scratches that could cause shuddering or skipped sections of any track. Henry's Records were invited to a special launch of the new technology at the Holiday Inn in Sloughby Polygram Records, a company that had been formed by the amalgamation of the Philips, Polydor and Decca Record companies. After drinks and nibbles we were ushered into a darkened room for the presentation which featured several samples of the mind-blowing new digital sound including Vangelis: 'Chariots Of Fire', Dire Straits: 'Love Over Gold', Roxy Music: 'Avalon', and not forgetting the inevitable Richard Strauss: 'Also Sprach Zarathrustra from the movie '2001, A Space Odyssey'. Even my old first ascendancy, King Crimson: 'In the Court Of The Crimson King', which was now on the EG label and part of Polydor.

I was absolutely blown away with the sound quality. Polygram did a really noble thing in those times of mass competition and rivalry. They decided initially that they would give exclusive distribution of this new media to a few hundred loyal dealers, including us of course. This meant that only certain branches of HMV and Virgin got to have compact discs at the beginning. As part of the deal, we received a Philips CD100 compact disc player, the first player to be released, to demonstrate CDs to our customers, along with compact disc display racks, manufactured by a company called Lift, which were very expensive to buy, plus a lot of in-store promotional and point of sale material. In return, we had to give them a substantial opening order of course, as well as committing to some advertising costs.

Polygram initially released one hundred and twenty titles – seventy five popular and forty five classical. So, for several months, we had virtual exclusivity of compact discs in Southampton but of course, it wouldn't last, as the inevitable pressure from the big boys and Polygram's desire to make as much money as possible opened the flood gates! CBS/SONY followed Polygram's lead in March 1983 with seventeen titles including Abba: 'Visitors, Michael Jackson: 'Thriller', Billy Joel: 'The Stranger', Simon and Garfunkel's 'Bridge Over Troubled Water', Barbra Streisand: 'Guilty', Bruce Springsteen: 'Born to Run' plus several jazz releases by Miles Davis, Weather Report, Herbie Hancock, Al Dimeola and John McLaughlin. It took CDs a good two years to take off though and it wasn't until the first digitally-recorded rock album (there had been classical ones) by Dire Straits, 'Brothers in Arms' was released in 1985 that sales went literally through the roof. 'Brothers' became the first CD to sell over a million, still being the third biggest selling CD of all time.

In 1982, I was going out with a girl that worked at Southampton's General Hospital. Both of us decided to take part in the annual Southampton hospitals' charity 'Bed Race', as well as promoting the shop as part of the fun. Each team had a theme, dressing up accordingly, with our suitably named 'Henry's Records Music Express' team including six record company reps dressed up as people representing various music genres. Steve Foord, the Polydor rep blacked up to become a Rastafarian representing reggae (one can only imagine the 'outrage' if seen in modern 'politically correct' times!) One must remember that this was part of the culture in those times, and never intended to be 'offensive', with the biggest applause and laughs coming from the Afro-Caribbean crowds who lined the streets as we all passed by.

EMI's Steve Waters portrayed a kaftan-wearing hippy, with flowers, beads, bells, with Pye's Nick Hugg as a rocker dressed in jeans and leather jacket, alongside RCA's Tony the 'Punk Rocker'. Each team borrowed an old hospital bed to dress up, with our effort covered in old LP record sleeves. It was then a mad race with all teams pushing their fancy-dressed beds through a set course on the streets of Southampton, starting out at the city's other hospital, the Royal South Hants.

That same year, I was invited back to the Concorde Club to take part in their 25th Anniversary week. There was one memorable night when all of the past disc jockeys were invited back for one big disco night featuring us all. There were seven of us in all, and I think that the only one missing was Simon Peterson's original partner, Jon Ferris who had run the popular Imperial Ballroom in Market Street Eastleigh. By this time, Joe Craen had relocated to East Anglia, but made the long arduous journey back especially for it, with a nice little piece featured in the Echo.

By November 1983, the larger competitors were having various effects on us. First of all, HMV relocated to new premises, four times the size of their Bargate store, which was a bit too close to us for comfort. Virgin had expanded to bigger premises. Then in December 1983, Pete Bentley left Henry's to take over as outright manager at Eastleigh's Jack Hobbs Records. The other full time staff member at the time was Warren Costa, son of Sam and Julia who ran Southampton's premier live pub venue at The Joiners Arms, just down the road from us in St Mary St. We'd had a whole wealth of Saturday assistants during Pete's time including DJ Joe Craen, Kevin Haynes, my sister, Marie Clare, Dean Dalrymple, former full time assistant Steve Crimble and Carl Maskelyne. On Christmas Eve 1983, after the store had experienced its best ever seasonal trading, we held a Farewell / Christmas party for Pete after the store had closed to which all the past and present staff members who had worked with Pete (and some that had not) were invited. A new team started after Pete's departure, with ex-Virgin records assistant, Pete Stock taking over as the main singles buyer assisted by an extremely likeable young man called Gary Blackman, while Carl Maskelyne continued as our Saturday lad.

A booze-fuelled party night (Pete on the right) with lower pic showing me, Carl Maskelyne, Vince, Warren Costa and Pete

L-R Steve Crimble, me, Pete, Arthur Richfield, Henry with Dean Dalrymple and Paul 'Vince' Vincent in front.

1983 saw the publication of the fruits of my labour of love, following a couple of years of hard slog around the live gig circuit, whereby I enjoyed the local bands as well as interviewing them. Assisted by Terry Hounsome, we catalogued comprehensive lists of the various line-ups, many of which changed across many years. We produced the large heavy ring-binder of hand-written A4 sheets with in-depth information, along with many rare photographs of the groups. A smaller type-written copy was later issued, being photocopied by several people in the area, so a few of these are thankfully still around.

As you will probably be aware - the main original files are now in the safe hands of David St John, who added a webpage labelled 'Southern Roots'. He plans to publish another book later in the year as a follow-up to his first account of his own early years in the entertainment game (SR 1 for short). SR2 will see much of his 'Groups' web-pages content carried across into book form. We only undertook this project for fun back then but glad to see that some of it has been shared on the internet ever since. Better still when seeing the spin-off book published nearly forty years on!

More memories of Pete can be found near the end of the story. 1984 was a major year in my life, with two significant events. First of all, I married Henry's niece Linda, so really becoming part of the family. This actually confused some of our customers who'd always assumed that Henry was my father! It used to highly amuse me when people used to come in and say *"Is your Dad here?"* with my reply of *"No, sorry. He's at work at Eastleigh Loco works!"*. Linda and I were married at Southampton Registry office on September 21st with a blessing at All Saints church, Botley on the following day, with Bob Pearce as my best man. It was the best day of Henry's life, as he'd always regarded me as the son that he never had, as well as virtually raising Linda like his own daughter. For the two people that he cared about the most, to actually be setting up life together was like a dream come true, and needless to say, we are still together now, and it has been a great marriage. Amazingly, we really disliked each other when we were teenagers- if anybody had told us then that we'd have ended up marrying each other, we'd have laughed them out of the shop!

Even now, we often look back at these old photos to reminisce over our wonderful times together as we built up the shop's reputation, giving us a golden opportunity to meet so many people across the counter. Many of us are still in touch, sharing the stories of where life's path took us long after the closure with the bonus of reuniting with many more thanks to the advent of social media. Quite often, someone somewhere in the world does a little search on a name, only to find a link to the very person on a website or on Facebook. We never dreamed about this back in the days of Henry's Records - it would have labelled science fiction at the time, although I often predicted that the new fangled computers would eventually enable mass communication on an unprecedented scale. This germ of an idea was sprung when the record companies introduced this technology for ordering purposes, as it was obvious that inputting basic data was a small step to what evolved into the internet.

Our wedding day, and next day's blessing with Best Man Bob Pearce and our daughter Sunita.

Our next main event was deciding to completely re-furbish the shop, as we owned the premises at 116 St Mary St anyway. The old wooden floorboards were in a bad state of disrepair, with one spot, being so rotten that we were in danger of losing a customer down into the cellar at any minute! The old wooden front shop window frames were full of dry rot and mildew. We completely replaced the floor with cheaper, but more resilient particle board with carpet tiles on top and had a brand-new aluminium-framed shop front, including a retractable pull-down security shutter. On the old shop front, due to the ever-present threat of vandalism, we'd had wrought iron security grills which had to be taken down, stored all day, and then put up again and padlocked at each end every night. The new shutter was much simpler. At the same time, having two floors upstairs that were not being used, we decided to gut the old backroom workshop/staffroom downstairs, to extend the shop to create more room for the growing CD business, creating a proper staffroom and office upstairs.

The downstairs extension became the classical music dept with a bit more seclusion for classical buyers to listen to music without having to compete with the more raucous sounds coming from the front of the shop. We had a really interesting time gutting out the back room because, as the workmen were stripping off the various layers of wallpaper on the walls, they found copies of newspapers from 1934. They were remarkably, fairly intact, having obviously been used as a form of cheap insulation in those days, so made for very interesting reading. It was a very stressful time during the refurbishment, disrupting the business significantly, especially considering that we could only trade off half of the shop at once, as the floor was being ripped up. The entire front of the shop was hoarded up, with customers entering over a temporary plank of wood, through a make shift wooden door. This was my first experience at project management, putting ME in good stead for my future retail career when later leaving these shores for a new life on the other side of the world.

Apart from promoting the national recording stars, we never overlooked our own home grown talent, especially when they released any new recordings. One such outfit was a studio band fronted by Trevor Cummins, named Close Shave who released a single on the New World label in 1981. 'It Don't Hurt Anymore' didn't make a big impact on the charts but sold fairly well in our area, following one of our well-liked window displays as seen here.

It was a very expensive renovation, but ending up with virtually a pristine, brand new shop. However, if we'd have known what was going to happen in the next few years, we might have saved our money. At the same time that we were making changes to our shop, Southampton City Council was promising to do great things in the way of upgrading St Mary Street. They planned on spending around £500,000, with talk of planting trees right down the middle, helping tenants to renovate their shops. The old Kingsland Market would be revamped to become undercover, as well as creating more residential property in the area by building smart new townhouses. Unfortunately, most of it never came to fruition, apart from a few ideas that happened long after we were able to benefit from it. The one thing that they did do, as part of some great plan to make St Mary Street a standalone shopping precinct, was to redesign the traffic flow at the Six Dials roundabout end. This made it very difficult for customers to actually find St Mary St, yet alone get into it and having the opposite effect to business.

Our final team with me, Ashley Field and Ian Hutchins.In 1985, the staff turnover saw Ashley Field, the son of a friend of the family, becoming my second in command along with a new junior assistant Ian Hutchins. Sadly, these were the last two paid staff members with Henry's Records, apart from one more Saturday lad – Steve Friend. Our last personal appearance by a recording artist took place around the same time, as Gary Moore had just released an album on Virgin titled 'Run for Cover'. The former lead guitarist with Thin Lizzy had now embarked on a solo career, undertaking a promotional tour of the national record shops.

The artist p.a. circuit had largely become pretty well the exclusive property of HMV during the late Seventies/Eighties, but Gary, even though, he was a Virgin recording artist, kindly insisted on visiting the 'real independent' record shops. Therefore, the Virgin rep had no option but to bring him to Henry's, being one of the lucky few.

We were celebrating thirty great years at that time, despite the growing realisation that time was running out for us all in the face of the overwhelming competition. Henry never stinted on advertising from the early days, some examples having been included in this book.

HENRY'S RECORDS

WE'RE 30 YEARS OLD THIS WEEK!

We've been selling Great Music from the days of 78s to today's Compact Discs

And we still have our reputation for stocking a more interesting and varied range of music

For the Best in Jazz, Blues, Soul, R & B, Folk, Country, Rock 'n' Roll and Nostalgia

Plus a wide range of Compact Discs

HENRY'S RECORDS
The Specialist Record Shop

116 St. Mary Street, Southampton
Tel. Soton 229230

**PURVEYORS OF GOOD MUSIC FOR 30 YEARS
1956 to 1986**

CHAPTER TEN – THE END OF AN ERA

Then another hammer blow arrived, leading to a new and devastating turn for our business. W.H. Smith took over a chain of record stores called Our Price Records, which had started with a few independent record shops, rapidly expanding to a great number of outlets. As part of the further expansion, Smiths in their infinite wisdom decided to open not one Our Price shop in Southampton - but two! As can easily be deducted from the shop's name, their focus was all about lower prices, resulting in a cut-price war. With Our Price selling chart and top name albums and singles at bargain basement prices, Virgin and HMV were not going to be outdone, as the price war escalated to epic proportions with those highly desirable albums now being available to the public at literally cost price (and sometimes below!).

We were faced with a dilemma with two immediate choices. Either join in, therefore totally eroding our profits, giving us less revenue to pay the bills, wages etc. Or just let them get on with it, give that business away and not stock chart or top name albums or singles anymore and specialize even more. We chose the latter. This meant that we were deliberately and intentionally giving business away, a big gamble, but as we weren't making any money on it anyway, it was no loss really.

It meant that the few faithful disc jockeys that were still buying from us had to go elsewhere, as we were no longer selling new release singles. We kept selling the Top 30 chart singles mainly to keep supplying the juke box companies, and because we were one of the shops that supplied data for the British Record Music Bureau. They compiled the National Top 40 singles chart bringing all sorts of free benefits for us (not that we ever fiddled any of our chart sales data!).

As for our chart album business, we'd already lost it to the high-profile chain stores, apart from our incredibly loyal customers who were still prepared to pay more to buy from us! We now focused more than ever on the specialist fields of jazz, blues, folk, country, reggae, soul and R&B, classical, world music and indie. Our customer bag was recreated again to reflect our new speciality focus, designed once more by Bob Pearce. We then embarked on a fairly extensive advertising campaign to re position ourselves in the market, using the independent magazines, 'Ear To The Ground' and 'Due South' plus specialist magazines like 'Folk On Tap, Folk Roots, Jazz Journal, Blues Unlimited' plus the Echo of course. The suppliers that we were doing the most business with now were Discovery Records, Celtic Music, Projection Records, Swift Distribution, Pinnacle, Rough Trade, Stage One (still), Conifer, Spartan, H.R. Taylor, Jazz Horizons, Charly, Jetstar, VJM, IRS (Chris Wellard), JSP and Pacific. We avoided the major record companies, apart from limited dealing with them, to obtain the specialist labels that only they distributed. These being Bluenote, Verve, ECM and Sonet plus the top name jazz, folk, country, blues, soul/reggae artists that recorded for major labels such as Miles Davis, Richard Thompson, Robert Cray and Bob Marley to name a few. So - in one foul stroke overnight, all of the major record company reps stopped calling on us.

The first couple of years (85/86) of this new direction were fairly successful, gaining more and more support from small local organizations like the Southampton Jazz Society and The Fo'csle (Folk) Club, but the really worrying issue was the decline of the street. St. Marys Street soon took on a 'run down' appearance as the small traditional shops moved out, with a less salubrious influx of tatty second-hand shops, Asian delis and take-way outlets plus a couple of sex shops. This all added to the deterioration of its previous character, as people avoided the seedy area which by now had little to offer.

We seriously looked at relocating, investigating properties in Bedford Place, East Street and even Ocean Village by the old Docks. However, the extortionate rents were all ridiculously high, so as we owned 116 St Mary Street - we stayed put for a while. In spite of our brave attempts to re-position ourselves, the writing was on the wall by 1987. We just were not generating enough income to put any money in the bank. It was a case of (just) keeping our heads above water, still paying the bills but there was no longer any profit in it. April was a particularly grim month, only taking £800 in one week (our normal average week was around £1250, so it had dropped by over 40%. The year before, our average week had been £3,500! In April 1987, we actually made a loss that month of £1600, the likes of which had been unheard of. With our backs to the wall, we sadly had two drastic choices. Firstly, beginning to cut costs, and everybody who is in business knows that the first thing that you cut is the wages. We regrettably decided to lay off our two staff members, a very heart-breaking decision as Ashley was the son of a friend of the family and music was his life. To his credit, 'Ash' had no ill feeling at all, as the job had become pretty boring due to the lack of customer footfall with relevant low takings of around £70 on some days.

Ironically, I gave him an application form for a trainee managers course with HMV, as well as putting out feelers for a job with Virgin, those very two shops that had become one of our main reasons for being in this predicament now. Ash had an interview with Paul Brixey at HMV, a second one with the Regional Manager plus another interview with Steve Pullen, Regional Manager of Virgin (formerly Store Manager of the Southampton store) who eventually gave him a job in their Portsmouth shop. My wife, Linda and I then decided to run the shop by ourselves, with no extra wages, as she came in from 10.30 to 2.30 in between the school run for our daughter. Steve Friend helped out on Saturdays, so we managed as best as we could in the face of these difficult times. Henry was still coming in every day, but his life had always been one of social interaction with customers who were now thin on the ground. He would then disappear over to the Kingsland Tavern at 11.00 am each day to catch up with his boozing mates, come back at 3pm to sleep it off in the office upstairs in time to sober up to drive home!

The other choice in cost-cutting was to cut our buying to the quick, which was a 'Catch 22' because if you didn't have it, you couldn't sell it! There was only one heart-breaking choice left for us – to sell the business as a going concern based on our well-respected profile, before losing any more money. We advertised it in various business real estate publications such as Daltons Weekly, Luxton & Lowe, plus music industry magazines like Music Week. We only ever had two groups of people come to look at it, and I'm sure that they would have been put off by the dire dirty dilapidated sight of St Mary St before they'd even walked in our door. So, finally in early 1988, we had to make the hardest decision of all and sell it all off individually and close it down. We started selling all of the stock gradually with lower discounts at first, gradually building up to bigger and bigger ones towards the end as the more desirable items had gone.

Most of the fixtures were sold to Weasels Second Hand Record Shop across the road, before selling the premises. We advertised the property ourselves this time without employing a real estate agent to cut down costs, leading to an absolutely ludicrous scenario taking place. Two Asian gentlemen, who both owned separate businesses in the same street were both interested. Frank owned the D.I.Y. shop, with Joe owning both the garage in the back corner of Kingsland car park, as well as the café on the corner, diagonally opposite us. I finally seemed to have a deal with Frank as he rang me to finalise on a good price of £37,000. Then the phone rang again soon after. Joe had somehow got wind of it, so asked me what Frank was offering? I told him, whereby he immediately upped the price to £38,500. I phoned Frank and he came straight to the shop to offer £40,000.

As soon I got back to Joe to tell him, his response was to match that price. To cut a long story short, I was left playing auctioneer with Frank in front of me, as the telephone bids were upped by Joe, who kept offering £500 more on each of his rival's price. Joe added £1,000 each time, with Frank's feverish £500 upping the stakes. Finally, Joe pushed his price up to £50,000, leaving Frank to begrudgingly bow out of this hilarious bidding war. As you can imagine, we were ecstatic at selling up for £13,000 more than anticipated, not forgetting our downward spiral over the last few months of falling figures on the balance sheet.

The sad last day of Henry's trading was Saturday 7th May 1988. LPs and cassettes were down to £1.99 each, or 3 for £5, with CDs priced at £2.99 each or 2 for £5, with singles at 25p each! At 2pm we knocked it all down again for the final time to £1 for LPs and cassettes (3 for £2), CDs at £1.99 (3 for £5) plus singles at 10p each (6 for 50p). By 5pm, all that we had left in the entire building were 2 LPs, 5 CDs and 30 singles. Our incredibly loyal customers had been buying any old rubbish just to say that they'd bought 'something' from the last day that Henry's was open. Phil Matcham, one of our regular customers called, insisting on buying the last ever LP sold at Henry's. As there were only two LPs left, he had to buy them both, not wishing to be outdone. Phil asked Henry and I to sign both covers, adding *"these are the last records ever sold in Henry's Record Shop – 7th May 1988"*

Phil, wherever you are mate…. have you still got them? I bet you do, and still treasure them, although if my memory serves me right, they were both instantly forgettable rubbish! We took £1,200 on that last day, as well as having a stream of local retailers who came to bid farewell with cards and gifts. In fact, the girls from TM Stores next door handed us a giant card signed by every trader in the street, plus more presents from a collection that they had made from everybody. I received an engraved Schaeffer pen, whilst the boss was given an engraved brandy hip flask plus an engraved pewter mug with 'Henry's Records 1956 – 1988'. It was all too much for poor old Henry who burst into tears at the outpouring of love and support shown by so many people. As you can imagine, this being one of the saddest days of my life, as it really was the end of an era.

The 'old' St Marys Street had a community feel, boosted by the nearby Kingsland Market whose stallholders all knew each other as did many of shop staff throughout the length of the busy street. Nowadays, the area is a shadow of its former self but remains as a wonderful memory for those who knew it back in those happy times. Henry and I often talked about how lucky we both were, in following our dreams which mirrored each other with our passion for music. He regularly went back to Cardiff, to meet up with family, friends, fellow staff as well as visiting his old haunts.

Henry's pewter mug

Linda and I had been looking at other businesses as early as March 1987. We originally had ideas of grandeur by taking over St Mary Street Post Office from Fred Hallam. His health was not good, so thinking of selling up around that same time. Post Offices are great little earners and always in demand, so possibly setting us both up for life. However, when Fred had it valued at £150,000, we knew that this dream would not be fulfilled as our premises were only valued at £40,000.

Another Post Office was on the market, along the coast on Portland Bill, so we made our way down to take a look at it. The final leg of this journey saw us stuck behind a refuse truck travelling down the small road to the Portland Bill location. It then dawned on us that we were close to the landfill tip for the whole of South Dorset as the stench drifted all over the area. We shivered as a howling cold biting wind came off the English Channel so knew that we couldn't work and live there for the foreseeable future. Another option was a bookshop in Devizes, as I had harboured thoughts of opening a Games and Pastimes shop from scratch as they were getting very popular by then. This didn't really work out, not forgetting my main passion for music which even - horror of horrors, saw me write to Virgin Records, enquiring if they needed any record shop managers! Luckily for me, they didn't, although I did have an interview in London on 5th August 1987.

CHAPTER 11. A LIFE-CHANGING DECISION

"Should I go or should I stay?" sang the Clash in 1982. Little did I know how that line would be buzzing around our heads a few years later as we weighed up our options. Life had been great for us, but all good things usually come to an end, especially for any small shops in the face of the massive onslaughts by the big players.

Australia had always loomed large in my mind, more so back in September 1986 when my wife Linda's best friends, Averil and Eamon flew over from Perth, Australia to stay with us for a while. Whilst enjoying a pub visit, I quizzed them about the whole way of life in that country, fuelled by television programmes such as 'Whicker Down Under' where Alan Whicker interviewed several ex-pat 'Poms'. Without exception, they all gave glowing reports on how wonderful it was, with no regrets apart from the obvious wrench of leaving family, friends and neighbours behind as they decided on the big gamble of their lives to relocate to the other side of the world.

The weather, scenery and general way of life was quite a contrast to the UK following the previous gloomy years of political strife and a general pessimism that hung in the air. We both knew in our hearts that this was the next big step, as well as being impressed with watching a section of 'Australia Live' on our TV screens. This was part of a four-hour telecast, broadcast live via their Nine Network on New Year's Day 1988 to open Australia's Bicentennial celebrations, two hundred years after the first settlers landed in Botany Bay. We were hooked.

I was the only family member without Australian citizenship. Linda had lived in Sydney for ten years during her previous marriage. Our daughter Sunita had been born there and our son, Mark had been registered as an Australian citizen when he was born, albeit in England. This, because he had an Australian mother, enabled me to obtain my visa - a mere formality with these cast iron family links.

The other big carrot was the fact that the exchange rate in May 1988 was $2.63 Australian Dollars to the pound. We could nearly triple our money at a stroke, with my share of the proceeds from the sale of the business and our house when sold. This high degree of solvency was fortunately a major contributory factor in being granted full Australian citizenship. It provided a huge opportunity to start another business there, as the country welcomed any kind of investment, offering government help where needed.

Our minds were made up, as I obtained my visa before deciding to arrange a big farewell Henry's night at the Botleigh Grange Hotel. We invited ex-staff members, some of our loyal disc jockeys, musicians, customers from over the years, to join our friends and family members. It was a good - albeit a sad night with mixed emotions as expected. We all looked back at the great times, with feelings of pride at having made a success of the shop until the large corporate entities bulldozed their way into the record retail business, forcing the closure of many small outlets.

The big day arrived on Wednesday 15th June 1988, as we flew off to our new life. I am often heard to say that moving to Australia was the third best decision that I ever made in my life. The first one was the day that I accepted that job at Henry's Records. The second one was marrying Linda, but if it wasn't for the first decision, the other two would never have happened. I would not have met the boss's niece Linda, as well as later to live in Australia.

I would never have had the pleasure to meet and get to know Henry Sansom, who was not only one of the best friends that I have ever had in my life, but more like a second father to me. The other major bonus was in meeting all of those wonderful customers, musicians, disc jockeys and staff members some of whom became great friends and still are, as many of us are still in touch across the miles. We naturally miss the beautiful city of Southampton and surrounding area, full of so many memories that will stay with us forever. This Henry's Record Shop story might have been lost in the mists of time, but the idea of writing it down had been buzzing around my head for many years. Better late than never as they say, so I trust that you have enjoyed reading about the finest record shop for miles around. It is fondly remembered by those who knew of it back in the day, often highlighted across the social media, especially on several Facebook pages that cover Hampshire's modern history and heritage. Just Google the name to find more of its place as a city landmark that disappeared along with many small shops that offered a personal service, unlike those of today.

I made a 'pilgrimage' back to my home town in 2003, spending time in hooking up with mates as well as a nostalgic walk along St Marys Street as the wonderful memories came flooding back. One of my good pals arranged a fund-raising party bash at the King Alfred pub just around the top corner, the proceeds of which helped toward my very expensive airfare! I cannot put into words what it was like on that day – the atmosphere and music will remain with me forever. I still thank them all to this day. This write-up has been in my files ever since so can reproduce it – hope to identify the scribe at some stage.

THE JOHN CLARE 'FARE HOME' BENEFIT SHOW!
The King Alfred P.H. Northam Road

19th January 2003- post gig report
(Author unknown)

For those with good memories, the name John Clare should stir the old grey matter into nostalgia mode and thoughts of buying real records in a real record shop! John was the manager at the much missed Henry's Record Shop in St Mary's Street Southampton, and when it finally closed, he emigrated to Australia.

Always one for attending gigs, especially those featuring his favourite artistes, John was known to travel here and there to see them. However - this has to be the ultimate- the re-formation of Love, a band from way back, just happened to be playing a couple of dates in the UK. They are also one of Mr Clare's all time top acts, so the decision was made. He was coming over to see them! Long way to travel to see a band you may think – you'd probably be right, but what if you could only afford a one way ticket? That was John's dilemma, but he travelled anyway because his good mate- photographer Ainsley Adams had suggested organising a benefit gig featuring all the musicians who knew John, to raise his fare home!

After one or two last minute venue changes, the musicians began to gather at the King Alfred around 4 pm, and although many of those invited were unable to be there, it was definitely a case of 'Spot the Muso'. Those present (some to perform – others to socialise) included: Arnie Cottrell, Damage, Steve Roberts, Pete Hunt, Bruce Roberts, Brian Wright, Joss Jones, Johnny Wands, John Picken, Mo Thomas, Beau, Bob Pearce, Pete Harris, Mick Steele, Rick Brown, John Lawrence, Sid Carter, Chris Parradine, Ray Drury, Harry Frith and many others. The place was really jumping!

The audience were treated (if that's the word?) to approximately forty five minutes worth of an 'Onslow Reunion' when Messrs Pearce, Harris, Roberts and Wright, augmented with the incredible Ray Drury, performed as if they'd never parted. Numbers included 'Everything's Gonna be Alright, Stranger Blues, Reeling and Rocking', and of course 'Hey Hey – The Blues Is Alright'.

Just how much was made towards John's plane ticket is not known, but then everybody had such a good time. Besides – we are sure he'll find a way home somehow. He always did- after a night out!

CHAPTER 12. ACKNOWLEDGEMENTS:

I'd like to thank several important people by personally naming them now (forgive me for any minor spelling mistakes). Sadly, some are no longer with us but their names live on – especially that of the well-loved staff member and close mate Pete Bentley. You will have read about his leaving party early in this story, following which he moved onto other record stores, but still keeping in touch long after. I last hooked up with him and many more old pals when I made the long trip back in 2003, including that amazing reunion at the King Alfred pub on Northam Road. Our last time together as shown here.

He passed away at the young age of 55 in October 2012, with a well attended funeral, followed by a lively uplifting wake with soul music, singing and even dancing which was a fitting tribute to his memory.

Our mutual friend Andy Lombardi sent a copy of this poignant image of Pete superimposed on one of the famous record bags from that time – a reminder of happier times.

You will have read part of the story, when Pete left our store to carry on with his later successes at other record shops. I have loads of photos taken on that crazy 1983 'Farewell Party' plus others so forgive my indulgence in adding a couple more. It's just a little tribute that I can include in this book and keeps his memory alive amongst many that had the pleasure to have known or worked with him.

More of the big Farewell Frolics on Pete's Leaving Party..

Pete Bentley carried on working with other local record outlets, including Domino Records where his great knowledge and friendly manner won him many more friends over his later years. This is one of my favourite memories of a much-missed character and one of my best mates ever.

STAFF MEMBERS:

Pete Batt, Glen Clothier, Malcom Jenks, Glenn Beaton, Pete Simmons, Tim Foad, Alan Wooller, Michael Stuart, Keith Harryman, Kevin Haynes, Joe Craen, Steve Crimble, Paul Vincent, Marie Clare, Arthur Richfield, Tony Fowler, Paul Joslin, Dean Dalrymple, Pete Bentley, Phil McCarthy, Warren Costa, Carl Maskelyne, Gary Blackman, Pete Stock, Ashley Field, Ian Hutchins and Steve Friend.

DISC JOCKEYS:

Johnny Dymond, Joe Craen, Carole Hamilton, Arthur Sheriff, Simon Peterson, Paul Brixey, Jon Ferris, Bob Deene, Chris Golden, Geoff Knight, Tommy Kaye, Mike Windsor, Dave Carson, Keith Rea, Dave Anthony, Mike Bishop, Jimmy Layne, Jon Bradley, Dave Walker, Dennis Brynner, Dave Van Sieger, Steve Quinn, Scott Kirkpatrick, Jimmy Warwick, Duncan Campbell, Mike Taylor, Nick Ceroli, Geoff Bartlett, Mike Jerrez, Mike Race, Dave Lester, Paul Mico, Mike Butt who used to come over from Norway about four times a year to buy records for his nightclub there, and probably loads more that I've forgotten. Here with the very talented Johnny Dymond, Carole Hamilton and Joe Craen.

RECORD REPS:

Dennis Tungate, Geoff Rhoden, Brian Flynn, Bernie Skerratt, Nigel Tungate, Mike Gardner, Steve Waters (EMI), Fil Towers, Lew Hughes, Roger White (Decca), George Page, Mike Sage, Bill Groves, Dave Tweed, Peter Foote, Steve Foord, Phil Clift (Phonogram/Polygram), Len Carpenter, Jim Evans, Bob Lewis, Gerry MacLeod, Richard Moore, Richard Comben, Alvin Jordan, Pete Gibbins, Mark Finland, Malcolm Highmore (CBS), Mike Vincent, Nigel Heywood (RCA), Bob Willis, Pete Gifford, Steve Robinson, Nick Hugg (Pye), Mike Jeffries (WEA), Stu James, Steve Foord, Dave Terry, Paul Turner (Chrysalis/Arista), Mike Lawrence, Neil Storey, Brian Stephens (Island / Virgin), Mike Cox (Discovery), Duncan Titcombe (DJM), Dave Fryer (Relay), Robbie Day (IRD), Brian Harrison (Bush and St Clair), Nick Anstey (Stage One), Bert Fry, Patricia Kirk (Lugtons), Geoff Travis (Rough Trade), Dave Robinson (Projection) and I'm sure that there are more that I've forgotten.

And last but most importantly of all:

THE REGULAR LOYAL CUSTOMERS:

The Juke Box companies:

Derek Rowles, Graham and Reg (Autoplay), Herbie Katz, Lyn Davidson (aka Jane) and Ron (Liberty Coin), Mike Wilson, Terry and Cookie (Displaymatics), Reg Bicknell, Marion Feltham, Glenda and David St John (Revis Automatics), Southampton Jazz Society members, Skip Conway, Big Ron and Daisy Edwards, Fo'csle Folk Club members, Bob Crease, John Edgar Mann, Dave Williams and Jon Wicher, Musicians who became regular customers, Bob Pearce, Arnie Cottrell, Pete Harris, Carl Leyland, Bing Lewis, Don Cooper, Martin White, John Picken, Sid Carter and Beau.

Miscellanous names such as Rae Prescott, Steve Hewitt, Trevor Merrett, Tim Chambre, Salena Jones, Geoff Wall and Phil Tyler of Stick It In Your Ear', Phil Matcham, John Littlefair, Mick the Northern soul collector (never did know his second name!), John Isaacson, Lou Christie, Sid Wellard, Andrew Wolfe and Dave Wendes (who both became close friends), Richard Williams (later a Southampton councillor) and Paul Clarke from Radio Glen. Mr Bevis (our best classical music customer) and a gentleman that came in every Saturday for years and spent a fortune, but we only ever knew him as Mr.Matthews.

I still miss the record business every day and have always stayed an absolute music fanatic and avid collector all my life. Those were some wonderful times at Henry's, and I shall cherish them and the memory of Henry Sansom for the rest of my years. If any of the names throughout this story strike a chord with you, dear reader, then please feel free to contact David St John via his website. Future editions can be amended, edited and update thanks to the immediacy of Amazon publishing. Furthermore, he often passes messages onto me in the possibility of reuniting old acquaintances, so I look forward to this offshoot of finally getting this into print.

This story doesn't quite end here as our new lives took a major turn after much consideration. In the UK, we had few prospects of remaining in the record business that had dominated our lives, as well as being pessimistic about the state of the country in general. Australia had been constantly in our thoughts as we both looked at the pros and cons of emigrating – especially to the furthest corner of the globe. It was to be a massive wrench to leave Southampton, our family and friends, but our shared optimism about life in that beautiful country overtook these feelings. Hundreds of thousands of Poms had made that same decision in the past, with seemingly few having many regrets. It was – and still is - the land of opportunity, so were ready to take the big gamble by selling up and boarding a ship headed for our new destiny.

CHAPTER 13. WHAT HAPPENED NEXT

We arrived in Perth on 7th July 1988, firstly spending two weeks in Sydney with Linda's Dad, Ron and his second wife, Kaye and Linda's stepsisters, Tracey and Anita. Then stayed with Linda's best friend Averil and her husband, Eamon with their four children in Como, South Perth. It was a bit cramped, but beggars couldn't be choosers. Averil and Linda had been best friends since they were eleven in Chandlers Ford, going all through school together. Linda had first sailed out to Australia in 1968 to see her father, a few years after he had split up with her mother. Averil joined her for a holiday, never dreaming that she would meet her future husband onboard the same ship, then staying and settling in Sydney. Linda followed suit after a few more trips back and, forth by which time Averil and Eamon had relocated to Perth in 1987. They felt that Sydney, like many big cities in the world, had various inherent problems and was no longer a good place to bring up young kids.

Perth was still a quiet little developing city with pristine beaches and a lovely laid back, carefree lifestyle, as well as being absolutely full of ex-pat Poms! As Linda's best friend lived there, and we didn't know anybody else in Australia, plus we had young kids aged two and seven, we decided that Perth was the place for us as well. In hindsight it was a brilliant decision, because it is still wonderful and relatively unspoilt, being the second most isolated city in the world, very convenient when international pandemics are about!

My intention was to open another record/CD shop. We had come away with a fair bit of money from the sale of the business having owned the Southampton premises as well as the sale of our house. The exchange rate at the time was $2.63 Australian to the pound, so we nearly tripled our money.

I then started looking at both music stores for sale as going concerns, as well as empty shops to start from scratch. At the same time, I was visiting all of the local shops and asking them if they had any job vacancies. 78 Records, Dada Records and Wesley CDs. (All gone now). No joy though. I looked at record shops for sale in Gosnells (I didn't know then that it was one of the worst suburbs in Perth, as far as poor people and drunken aborigines go) and Nedlands, which was the exact opposite, extremely affluent and full of millionaires. After looking at the financial records, Nedlands looked quite promising, until a friend of Eamon's told me that the large nearby University had opened their own record shop. That was probably why the owner was deciding to sell, as the student population would have represented a huge slice of his clientele. Inside information is so valuable. Then I saw this great little shop in Kardinya (another lowlier suburb, which I had no idea about at the time). In a fit of impulsive eagerness, I put a bid in for it. I went to see the agent and had to sign a purchasing agreement.

During this time I had been visiting other existing record shops in the suburbs, especially a really good one at Dog Swamp Shopping Centre in Tuart Hill, run by a great English guy called Brian, who had known some of the same record reps in England that I knew. I ended up working a couple of days there as a volunteer, to get to know what the customers were buying. Luckily, thanks to Brian, he put me on to his financial advisor who told me not to buy anything without getting him to look at the finances first. His name was Bill Hicks, a fantastic guy who was a Cockney London East Ender. Luckily for me, Bill had told me not to sign anything unless I had clearly written as a condition of purchase: 'Subject to my financial advisor looking at the financial records and advising me that he thinks that it is financially viable'.

When I eventually got the books from the Kardinya business and presented them to Bill, my worst fears were confirmed. He gave me several pieces of advice. No.1: Don't touch it with a barge pole. No. 2: Buy a house quick because there was a property boom on, with prices going up and up, soon to be through the roof. No.3: If I was going to have a music business, then start my own from scratch because a lot of commercial Real Estate agents would take advantage of gullible, newly-arrived English guys like me and would rip me off. I went back to the agent to pull out of the deal who gave me a world of grief, because I had actually signed a purchasing agreement, but that clause that Bill had got me to write in saved me. Bill said that because of that, I could take him to court and win. I relayed this to the agent by phone, who begrudgingly relented by cancelling the deal after a real struggle, as well as taking a long time to get my 10% deposit back!

After that, I started looking at empty shops in suburbs with the unusual names of Innaloo (who would want to own a shop IN A LOO!), Balcatta, Girraween, Koondoola, Balga, Noranda and Wanneroo, all indigenous names of course, but I really didn't know what I was doing. Then Averil cleverly suggested that I apply for various jobs, work a year during which I could really get to know Perth. Learn where the good and bad suburbs were, as well as building up some knowledge of the city. I applied for lots of jobs, but not even getting interviews. This started a terrible two or three week period where I wasn't sleeping at night. I was scared stiff that I'd get no job - wouldn't be able to start a viable business, as well as suffering from culture shock, alienation and feeling like I didn't belong here. It does take a lot of courage in re-locating a young family to the other side of the world, even if you did have a fair amount of money. In the meantime, we bought a house, as prices were indeed escalating. We wanted to be within a reasonable distance of the beach, whilst being near the countryside so that our daughter Sunita, could go horse riding. At the same time, I didn't want to spend a fortune, wanting to keep as much capital as possible to start the business. Wanneroo was the ideal place (not to be confused with Waroona where we live now). It was relatively cheap, being way north of the city, but by having our first home along with buying a cheap little Mazda 121 which was economical to run, this really lifted my spirits.

The day after we signed the house contract, I had a very welcome phone call from Myer Department Stores, inviting me in for an interview. Myer was part of the Coles Myer dynasty, at the time, the fourth biggest retail organization in the world. It included US franchises K-Mart and Target, with outlets all over Australia and the

G.J Coles supermarket chain, started by an Australian entrepreneur. Myer had been started up by Russian immigrant, Stanley Myer with incredibly upmarket prestige stores having shops all over Australia. At the time, they had ten stores in Western Australia, but the job on offer was at the furthest store away from Wanneroo at Cannington, which was unfortunately as far south of Perth as Wanneroo was north!

The job on offer was running the record/CD bar as they called it (there are lots of Americanisms in Australia) due to the girl currently doing the job going on maternity leave. The store Manager, John Curtis was - guess what - a Cockney London East Ender, in fact, as I later found out, originally a barrow boy. After interviewing me, reading my CV and sussing out that I'd run my own business, he told me that I was overqualified to run the CD bar and that I was really management material. He told me to go and have lunch in the shopping centre food hall, then come back in an hour. By the time I got back, he had promoted one of his managers to the Perth City store, moved another manager to a different department in the store. He then offered me the job of manager of Home Entertainment, which included – yep - the CD bar plus televisions, Hi-Fi, video recorders, portable audio, computers, printers, phones, cameras etc. I knew nothing about any of this, but the money was phenomenal at $56,000 (around £32,000 p.a.) with 4 days off every other weekend plus four weeks paid holiday a year. In the nineteen odd-years that I'd worked at Henry's, and working for myself, I'd had about five holidays! Why the hell would I want to run my own business when I could have all of these perks!

Thus began three years of three hours total travelling time (there and back) every working day. It was a good job we'd bought an economical car that was cheap to run. After only a week in the job, I was in a mess psychologically again. I was full of self-doubt, lacking confidence and considering whether I was able to cope with the pressure of managing fifteen staff, working for a business that generated half a million in turnover per annum. I talked to the HR Manager, suggesting that it would be best for me to run the CD bar because I knew nothing about the other products and I'd only ever got myself a retail job in the first place, because I loved music! He said that he would talk to some people and come back to me. That afternoon, he came back with another department manager by the name of Trish Fretwell. She was the one that was about to be promoted to the Perth City store, but had another three weeks until she moved there. Peter Green, the HR Manager said that she was going to take over as my trainer for the next three weeks, so asked me to stick with it for that short time to see how I went and before coming back to me.

Thankfully, Trish taught me how to be a manager in a large department store environment, as opposed to a little privately owned record shop. She told me that I didn't have to fully know about any particular product because I had expert sales specialists, whose job it was to know about that and sell it. Of course, at Henry's I had always been the one with all of the product knowledge, so I naturally thought that that should still be the case! She taught me that the job of a manager was to delegate tasks, (hard for somebody coming from his own business. I had always done everything myself) as well as managing the people (I could do that). I had to ensure that we had stock on hand in the quantities that we needed (I could do that), manage the merchandising standards and housekeeping of the departments so that it always looked immaculate (that was new, but I reckoned that I could do that). On top of this to ensure that all policies, procedures and occupational health and safety rules were followed (new but I could learn that). Then, as time went along, I would naturally learn a bit about the product too (which I did) but never to the expert levels of my sales specialists. It was the start of a massive amount of stuff that I learnt in the nineteen years whilst at Myer, through various management levels, ending up as State Store Development Manager, responsible for opening new stores and refurbishing old stores. They were a brilliant retailer then (not so much now sadly) and their training was second to none. I know that I would never have developed the skills, expertise, knowledge and attributes which I now have, had I stayed in my closeted little world in England.

CHAPTER 14. A BIG TURNAROUND

Sunday 19th February 1989. The weather was really, unbearably hot, I'd just come through my first absolutely mental January Stock Take sale and was incredibly homesick. We took the kids to an idyllic beach at Lancelin, way north of where we lived, and I sat on the beach and took this photo of paradise, white sand, turquoise sea and azure blue sky and I'd never been more miserable in my life!

I wanted to go home....to England. Linda - as she always did and always has - supported my decision. I went to see John Curtis, the store manager. I'd only been working for him for five months having created the job especially for me. He called my Line Manager in, Carol Stace, another Pom, who was in charge of the whole of Home Leisure and Entertainment and asked her, in front of me, *"Is this bloke any good?"* Her reply *"He's absolutely brilliant"*. Then John turned to me: *"I'm going to say three things. Been there, done that, Two: Don't sell your house - rent it out because you'll be back! Three* (and this was the one that made me nearly fall off my chair) *"I'll keep your job open for you until stock take on June 20th. If you're not back by then, I'm advertising it.... but you'll be back"*.

We let the people that we bought the house from, come back in and look after it rent free, as they were waiting for a new house to be built. With the huge demand and backlog, it was taking them time and costing them a lot of money in rent. We had got to know them well through our mutual next-door neighbours, ending up becoming friends for life - in fact our best friends, with Mick being the closest thing that I've ever had to having a brother. So that was the first advantage of going back to England. We went back for three months.

We told our parents that we were homesick but didn't really know if we were coming back for good or just testing the water. After only a fortnight, we remembered all of the things that made us leave in the first place, the freezing cold (it was February), the pissing rain, the traffic queues, everything looked dirty. The people all looked miserable and grey from lack of sunshine. That holiday cost us $15,000 and it was the best money that we ever spent because when we came back to Perth, we've been really happy and content ever since. Furthermore, my confidence was by now sky high. I made another visit back to Blighty in 2003 – more of which later on.

Upon our return Carol told me that she wanted me to manage Toys and Sporting Goods, the busiest department in the store, through the Christmas period. I didn't like the way that it was laid out so asked if I could re-lay it all, ending up by moving it from one end of the store to the other in a busier foot traffic area. That was the start of me getting into Project Management which led me to managing the complete building of a brand new Furniture/ Electrical Superstore from the ground up. 15 years later - an $8m dollar project and I came in under budget!

After Toys, I was put into Furniture, a department with a reputation of being difficult to manage, with lots of problems but again my bosses had recognised that I had good trouble-shooting skills. I absolutely loved doing furniture, with the bonus of having a sales team of predominantly Poms from the North of England, and we never stopped laughing!

After 19 years, Myer made me redundant when the Coles Myer dinosaur (as it had now become) was split up, then sold off into separate companies, because it wasn't making a profit as a whole anymore. There were supposed to be no redundancy packages, and everybody was to be re-deployed in other parts of the company but there was no equivalent of my job, anywhere else and I held out and forced them to pay me redundancy. I was the only ex-employee to get it, much to the upset of many others, who took them to court and lost. It paid off my mortgage and helped me to retire at age 60. For the next few years, I had walked into a job at Salvos Stores, the retail division of the Salvation Army.

Like all of the other divisions of the Salvation Army, it had been run by a Salvation Army Captain, but then they thought, in their infinite wisdom, we know nothing about retail, let's bring in somebody that does. They appointed a guy called Alan Dewhirst as CEO, who had worked in every field of customer service, banking, retail, insurance, transport and he started bringing in retail experts like me. I absolutely loved it because now, I could use all of my forty years of retail knowledge and expertise to make money for people in need, instead of some bunch of Corporate Directors, sitting in an Ivory Tower somewhere, who make you redundant, in spite of your loyalty, after 19 years!

I gradually moved some of my ex-Myer mates into roles in the Salvos in Western Australia. and at one point - the entire W.A. management of Salvo's Stores W.A. was ex Myer. We transformed it into a proper retail organization with customer and merchandising service skills, plus high retail standards, doubling the amount of the cheque paid back to the Salvation Army at the end of the financial year within three years! I opened fifteen new stores for them, along with refurbishing ten others. It was not only very rewarding but really got me into an environment of helping people in need, so much so, that when I retired and moved to the little South West country town of Waroona, I was looking for something to do within the community and to help people, so joined my local Lions Club, in which I have been extremely active ever since. In conclusion, Australia has been very good to me. If anybody had told me some fifty years ago at Henry's that I'd end up in Australia, doing all of this stuff, I would have laughed them out of the room!

The people who later bought the record shop in Kardinya, went out of business a few years later. Then came the internet, Amazon and cheaper online CD purchases, followed by iPods, iTunes, Spotify, downloads and all manner of streaming music. If I had opened a record/CD store, I would have lost my shirt, over and over again. Kismet.

Henry's Records was unique and special, being a massively important part of my life, and I still relish it everyday, marvelling about how, time and time again, people still talk about it on Facebook sites, thirty odd years later. Often, I wish that I was still back there doing it, but it wouldn't be the same. The world has changed, and we all have to move on. Regardless, I would never have achieved in my life, what I have, by standing still. if I hadn't worked at Henry's Records. I would never have met my wife - never had my kids - never come to Australia or had the absolute honour of knowing and working with a man called Henry Sansom, who became one of the most special friends that I've ever had in my life - a second father to me. I hope that you enjoyed this book and that it brought back many special memories for you as well.

John Clare April 2021

CHAPTER 15. THE NEXT PHASE – THE MUSIC LIVES ON

A few doors away at no. 100a stood M&M Music, which started out in 1987, selling all kinds of musical equipment with great success. Run by Mick Williams and Mike Travis, catering for the local musicians, groups and the general public. Mick and his brother Bob (not part of the business) being well known in the area as top guitarists over many years with several top bands, including line-ups of the ever changing Bob Pearce Blues Band. 116 came back on the market later in 1988, which resulted in M&M moving into Henry's old premises.

Bob and Mick Williams above, with a small selection of guitars below.

The shop was then sold to fellow musicians Jamie Goatley and Tim Payne in 1992, who left in 2006. By 2008, Jamie decided to move out of the less than salubrious district, following attempted break-ins as well as not being able to open the store on one particular morning. The street was blocked off by a police cordon, following a murder which prevented many shop owners from gaining access. He recalls a 'strange vibe' at 116, with many unusual occurrences from time to time. On one occasion, he switched the upstairs lights off before locking the exterior doors, but looked up to see that they were still on. Another time he heard heavy breathing behind him, causing a rapid flight down the stairs and out into the street where he stayed for a while until a neighbouring shop owner kept him company as he slowly went back to check that all was secure. Also there was an occasional slight smell of cigar smoke around the shop, despite a strict no-smoking policy, so perhaps Henry's presence was still around? Who knows....

Tim's mother felt the atmosphere, feeling the need to 'exorcise' the property as she had experience in the supernatural. Her unorthodox method of saying prayers as well as sticking a pair of drumsticks in the shape of a cross on the wall seemed to have done the trick, putting an end to whoever – or whatever was making mischief! Strange but true.... Jamie kept the M&M name, incorporating it in the new 'Guitar Store' that opened in Commercial Road, still trading to this day. The shop front is one of the best I have ever seen, in the shape of a giant Fender amplifier – well worth a visit.

At the time of writing, 116 houses Extreme Electronics, a mobile phone/laptop sales and repair so the electrical link has carried on long after the Henry's Records years, albeit in much more advanced are of technology. John still keeps in touch with many of his UK pals, some of whom have got in touch with a few of their own recollections.

CHAPTER 16. THANKS FOR THE MEMORIES

Former staff and DJs have sent just a few of many memories – many more could probably fill another book.

Gethyn Jones writes:

It must have been the early to mid-1970s that I became aware of Henry's Records. Many of the record company promotion teams visited Radio Solent in the vain hope that we would play their latest releases! Henry's Records was also on their visiting list. Henry's was, I understand, one of the shops that submitted sales figures to the compilers of the UK Pop Charts. Therefore, they had more than their fair share of record reps pushing the latest tracks. These reps all had one thing in common – they all talked about this amazing guy at the shop with an encyclopaedic knowledge of new music. That guy is of course John Clare.

As presenter of the local radio rock show – I was focussed on featuring local musicians and bands – and good folk like John. John would join me on my show every week bearing an album and talking about the band or artist – usually someone new. I fondly remember John bringing in a record – Roxanne by Police before they were known and predicting big things. Well he wasn't wrong there.
In later years he was part of the team that comprised Oliver Gray and myself that put together a documentary series featuring all the famous and not so famous bands that emanated from the Solent area – Baked On The Premises (thank you Bob Pearce for the name). Great days and great memories.

Gethyn

PS Ask John to tell you about the VIP trip we had to see Bruce Springsteen's UK debut at Hammersmith Odeon. Limos and wacky backy!!!

Steve Gladders (DJ Steve Quinn)

Several abiding memories from Henry's Records for me. Here are a few. Firstly, John's astounding recollection of record catalogue/matrix numbers. Secondly, how busy the shop would be whenever a sale was on. Thirdly, going to the back of the shop (with fellow DJs Dave and Denis from the Coach House) to play that week's new UK releases and imports – and usually buying a fair few. Fourthly, going to the 'greasy spoon' café across the road (Rodrigo's?) for a fry-up. Egg, chips and beans never tasted any better!

Steve

Johnny Dymond DJ writes:

The magnificence of Henry's Records for a DJ, was that if they didn't have what you wanted a.s.a.p.- it was there within two days! Can't argue with that for service. Henry of course, along with John Clare, always went above and beyond. It was always the BEST record shop in Southampton

Ian Hutchins (former staff member)

None of you liked my choice in music. To be fair, looking back it was a bit poor apart from the Japan stuff. With age comes wisdom. I certainly expanded and improved my taste in music. Henry going to the bank with a bag of cash in the afternoon and popping in the pub. He was gone for ages. I used to fear for his safety sometimes. And the massive amount of Melody Makers and NME's stored in the office! Loved working there even if I didn't say it at the time.

Ian

DJ Joe Craen

Re Henry's, I remember that in the days when I worked in the shop, Henry would not allow me to work there if I had a beard. I have memories of sitting in the back room of the shop waiting for the chart to be read out at lunchtime on Radio One. Sadly, some years ago my file with all my entries into Henry's chart disappeared, either left at Hospital Radio or disposed of by my first wife.

Joe

Steph Crystal (ex staff- Steve Crimble)

Remember really well and felt so sorry, for anyone returning a faulty record after Henry had been to the pub, Henry would scrutinise and question the condition of the record, get his hanky out, wipe over the surface, whilst still smoking his cigar, dropping ash all over the surface!

The dinking machine - I wonder how many record centres I had punched out, including the Philips and Polydor hard centred singles, with the use of the kettle, with an adapted spout, to soften the centres, innovative and totally safe.... not......many burnt fingers! Polishing the floor, on hands and knees, the lovely red floor, felt so proud when finally finished. plus cleaning the outside windows, Ha Ha! John, playing on the outside speakers, "When I'm cleaning windows"... Just how busy we were at Christmas. Boxing Day lunch at Winchester, thank you Henry xx

All in all, what a wonderful time I had working there! Great staff and such fond memories that I'll never forget... And to think back, John you didn't really like my choice of music at my interview, but "hey ho" you gave me the job, the rest is history. Loved it

Steph

Dave Lester (Avenue Artistes DJ)

As a Southampton DJ, it was great to go to Henry's. They kept a box of the new releases there for us DJs to browse through. Henry was a great guy. R.I.P.

Dave

APPENDIX

PERSONAL PHOTOS AND MISCELLANEOUS ADVERTS ETC

(David St John)

John has kept a stack of photos since leaving our shores, some of which he emailed to me. A mix of Henry's early days in South Wales, leading to his moving to Southampton to eventually launch his first record shop. These great images portray the ever changing years in the music business, later enhanced when John came on the scene. When editing his fascinating account into this book form, it soon became apparent that there were far too many photos to include in the timeline within the confines of this book. You may have noted that my Henry's Records webpage was uploaded a few years ago so why not take a look?

www.davidstjohn.co.uk/henrys.html

He also keeps in touch with many old pals from those wonderful years, many of whom use social media to keep in touch to share. John wishes to give a special mention to Bob Croucher who owned Weasel's Second Hand Record Shop across the road from Henrys. Bob kindly sent John this old photo of the premises as both shops helped each other. They sent customers to each other, especially if odd discs had been deleted so there might be copies lurking in Bob's boxes.

Many former St Marys shoppers will remember these two shops as part of the experience back in the days when it was a pleasure to stroll down the busy road - especially when the Kingsland Market was operating. The pubs also did a roaring trade as one can imagine. As in several main streets in many towns and cities, the old community spirit is a thing of the past as they have long gone to be replaced by cloned shops with no character or decent staff who go the extra mile to fulfil any request. It was a pleasure to stroll up and down the road, often bumping into people you knew as well as finding free places to park, with the absence of meters or hovering traffic wardens etc.

The following superb images highlight Henry's musical talents in amongst a few pub crawls, when mixing with visiting record reps, customers and many friends who enjoyed his company throughout the best years. In addition you can read a few of the many adverts that were used to good effect throughout those ever changing times as the shop always stayed up with current trends, thinking ahead as the market moved into different tastes.

1984 caricature by Bob Pearce

One of Henry's famous liquid lunches at the Kingsland Tavern with old pals Bill and Bertie.

It has been a great pleasure to have read the story, as well as editing it all across into this publication, adding the relevant photos that help to bring it alive. Henry sadly passed away in March 1993 at the age of 75, with no surviving relatives around these days, apart from niece Linda (Clare). However, his memory lingers on as befits a talented musician, whose passion led to setting up his own store in 1956. Then followed by a fifteen year old musicologist who rose through the ranks to become a partner and a family member from 1969 until the close down. This was a match made in Heaven, so on behalf of thousands of record lovers over the Golden Years – we simply say in the words of ABBA:

"THANK YOU FOR THE MUSIC!"

David St John

Printed in Great Britain
by Amazon